DOTS INSIDE

Dots Outside

PAINT PENS

LINES INSIDE

BUBBLES

HEARTS

Flourishes

The KIDS' BOOK of HAND LETTERING

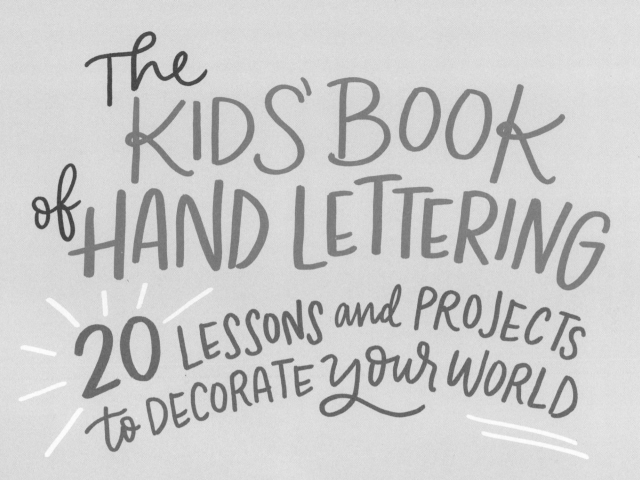

The KIDS' BOOK of HAND LETTERING

20 LESSONS and PROJECTS to DECORATE YOUR WORLD

BY:

Nicole Miyuki Santo

RP|KIDS
PHILADELPHIA

Running Press Kids
Hachette Book Group
1290 Avenue of the Americas, New York, NY 10104
www.runningpress.com/rpkids
@RP_Kids

Printed in China

First Edition: October 2018

Published by Running Press Kids, an imprint of Perseus Books, LLC, a subsidiary of Hachette Book Group, Inc. The Running Press Kids name and logo is a trademark of the Hachette Book Group.

The Hachette Speakers Bureau provides a wide range of authors for speaking events. To find out more, go to www.hachettespeakersbureau.com or call (866) 376-6591.

The publisher is not responsible for websites (or their content) that are not owned by the publisher.

Photography credit: Ikaika Pidot (Pidot Studios)

Print book cover and interior design by Susan Van Horn

We are grateful to the artists and makers who have allowed their work to be highlighted in this book. Permission to feature these pieces has been granted by Kiley Shai Photography (page 114), Pretty Branch Photography (page 194, top two images), and Winston Provisions (page 194, bottom image).

Library of Congress Control Number: 2017959766

ISBNs: 978-0-7624-6339-8 (paperback), 978-0-7624-6511-8 (ebook), 978-0-7624-6510-1 (ebook), 978-0-7624-6512-5 (ebook)

1010

10 9 8 7 6 5 4 3 2 1

CONTENTS

THIS BOOK
BELONGS TO:

_____

INTRODUCTION

Hey there! Welcome to *The Kids' Book of Hand Lettering*. Together, we'll walk through these pages, which are filled with lessons and projects to decorate *your* world—a world filled with family, friends, birthday parties, celebrations, fun accessories, and decorations that make you *you*.

Before you jump in, I have some good news. Did you know that you already have a head start learning hand lettering? Those letters you use every day to talk with your friends and family are the same letters we'll be using here. Instead of talking or typing, though, we'll be using our hands, putting pen to paper, to make your letters truly unique. Let's start your hand-lettering journey by writing your name on the previous page and owning this book.

Then, together we'll continue by diving into these lessons and projects so you can color your world and share with everyone you love!

HOW TO USE THIS BOOK

As you flip through these pages, you'll see lessons and projects paired together. Each mini-lesson consists of exercises and examples to help you learn how to turn your handwriting into your own unique hand lettering. Then, after each lesson, there is a fun project for you to make using your new skills—so get crafty! You'll soon have banners, party hats, wall art, gift tags, and more with your own designs!

This book starts by breaking down the letters and showing you how to make your hand lettering look fancy. Later, you'll work your way up to connecting letters, exploring your personal style, and using your hand-lettering skills for bigger projects, like wood art, tote bags, and balloons (yes, you can write on balloons!). I promise, it will be worth it for you to start with the first lesson and follow each lesson in order. Now, let's get started!

TOOLS + SUPPLIES

Hand lettering can be done with any pen—yep, that's right! You can use the pen you have in your backpack at the moment or the colored markers you have in your desk. The tools listed below are a few of my favorites and are the ones I will be using in this book.

LETTERING TOOLS TO TRY OUT:

o **Crayola Super Tips**

o **Crayola Broad Line Markers**

The thick tip is perfect for bigger projects.

o **Gel Pens**

o **LePens**

These small pens are great for smaller projects and don't smear!

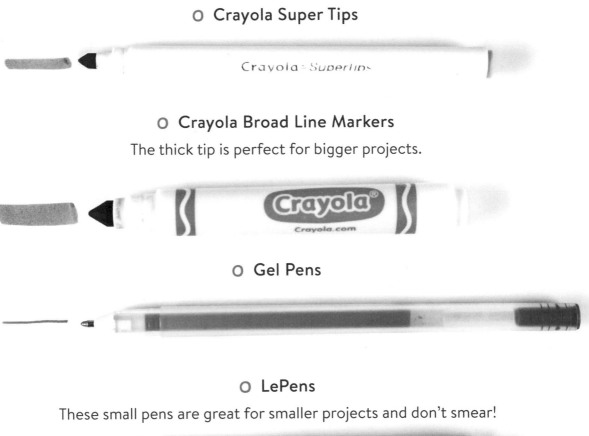

O Brush Pens

You'll learn more about these in Lesson 7. A few that I like are:

Tombow Dual Brush Pens

Pentel Fude Touch Sign Pens

O Paint Pens

You'll learn more about these in Lesson 11. Some brands to try out are:

Sharpie Oil Based Paint Markers

Sakura Pen-touch Paint Markers

Molotow Acrylic Paint Markers

MAIN SUPPLIES FOR THE PROJECTS:

- O Pencil
- O Scissors
- O Ruler

- O Hole Punch
- O Removable tape (washi tape and painter's tape)

- O Double-sided tape
- O String

The beginning of each project will also have a list of supplies you'll use to make that specific project.

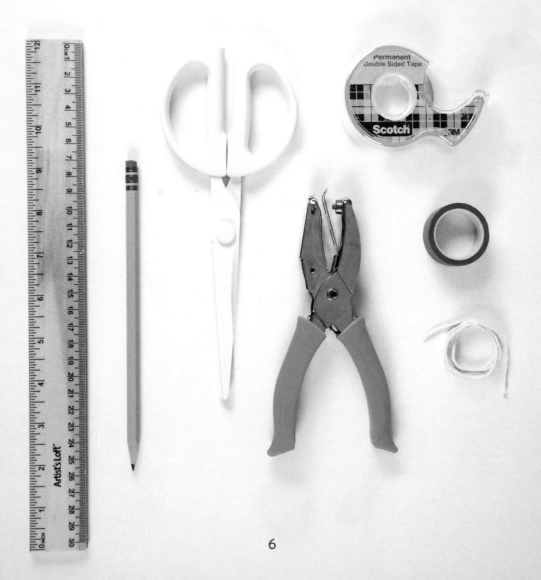

TYPES OF PAPER TO HAVE HANDY FOR THE LESSONS AND PROJECTS:

O **Scratch paper:** This can be computer paper, pages from a notebook, or any loose sheets you have lying around. I recommend using scratch paper for practicing.

O **Cardstock:** This thicker paper will be used to make the projects. You can purchase cardstock at art or craft stores. Ask for the paper section and have fun picking out your favorite colors!

O **Watercolor paper:** You'll use this in Lesson 5 when you learn about watercolors. A few of my favorite brands are Canson Watercolor Paper Cold Pressed 140lb and Fabriano Bright White Cold Pressed 140lb.

For a list of stores and online sites where you can buy your tools and supplies, check out the "Resources" section at the back of this book. There are so many options out there, and now is your chance to try any of them out. Now, let's get started and have some fun!

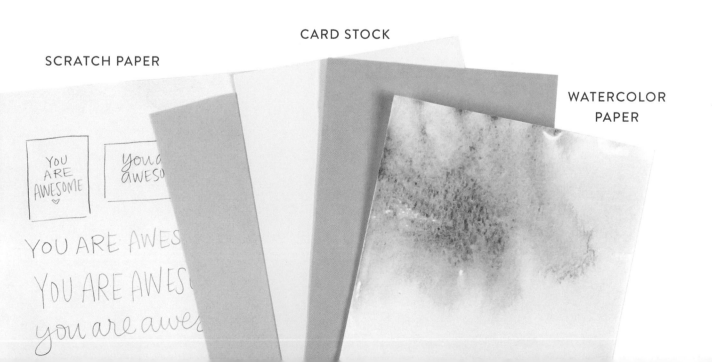

SCRATCH PAPER

CARD STOCK

WATERCOLOR PAPER

ON YOUR MARK, GET SET, LETTER

YOUR GRIP

Now that you have your supplies ready, let's get you set up. How do you hold your pen or pencil? At first, I'd like you to hold your lettering tool in your hand the same way. Then, here are a few pointers to help you feel confident and comfortable as you draw:

* Try to loosen your grip a little bit. It is common to grip your lettering tool tightly (like in the first photo below) to draw a perfect line. But perfect isn't what you're going for. Hand lettering is about expressing yourself, and it is harder to do that if you're tensing up. Try to grip your lettering tool a little looser, and your hand will thank you.

* However, try not to grip too loosely with your hand in the air (like in the second photo below). You might think a painter paints like that, waving a magic wand, but that's not the best way to draw your letters. Move your fingers closer to the tip of the pen and use a medium grip to feel supported and in control.

✳ As you go through the lessons in this book, I want you to try different ways of holding your pen. Experiment. This is how you figure out what works for you and also what doesn't work.

✳ To any of you who are lefties, you can absolutely hand letter too! When you have your paper in front of you, try rotating it to the right or to the left and see how that feels when you draw. You will need to experiment to find what is most comfortable for you.

WARM UP

Now, let's get your hands moving and ready to go. Draw little blades of grass like the lines below. Press down on the paper with your pen and then let go at the end. Draw these lines at different lengths and in different directions. They don't need to be perfect, and this is just your warm up! Fill up a full page, and then you can move on to our first lesson and project.

LESSON #1

FOUNDATION SHAPES

Here we are at your first hand-lettering lesson—super exciting! To begin, take out any writing tool you have handy in any color. Remember that it doesn't need to be anything special, as any marker or pen will work.

Looking at the lines below, can you see the different shapes and symbols? A circle, dash, curves, straight lines, and arches. They may be simple shapes, but they are powerful, as we'll learn later on. For your first exercise, draw each of these shapes on practice paper and copy them as you see below.

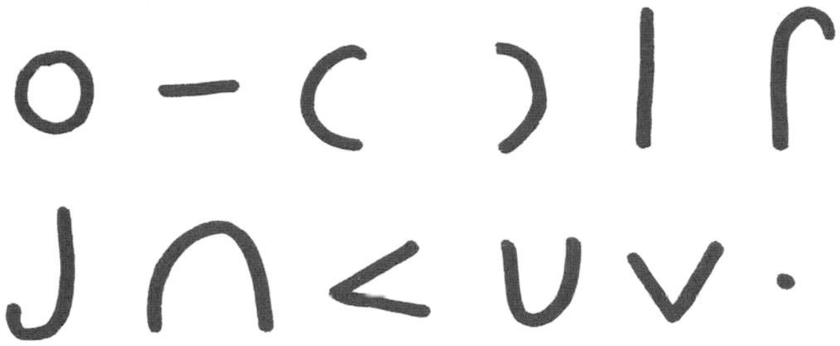

o – c) | ſ

ᒍ ∩ < ∪ ∨ ·

Then, draw two rows of just circles.

o o o o o o o o o

o o o o o o o o o

Next, try two rows of just dashes.

– – – – – – – – – –

– – – – – – – – – –

Continue drawing each shape multiple times. Then, experiment with making them smaller and bigger.

Now that you've got some practice, put your thinking cap on. What else do these shapes and symbols look like? Do you see a crescent moon or maybe a candy cane? Are there any other designs you can make by combining a few of these lines together? Try it out on your own. This will help get you prepared for your first project on page 14.

PROJECT#1
PATTERNS

It's project time! Do you have a school binder that needs decorating? Or is one of the walls in your bedroom bare, making the perfect canvas where you can showcase your art? Using the shapes you just practiced, let's add some pizzazz and fun to your surroundings.

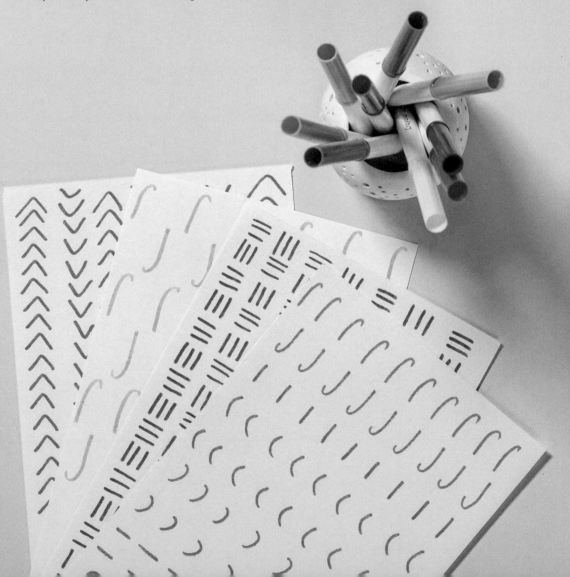

SUPPLIES:

O blank paper or cardstock

O any pen/marker

O scissors

O removable tape

1) Grab a few sheets of blank paper or cardstock and any pens you want to experiment with.

2) Draw the shapes and symbols you just learned and turn them into patterns. These can be one shape drawn over and over again or a mixture of shapes that, together, creates a new design. Below are a few ideas to jumpstart your fun pattern making:

- *Draw a group of dashed lines close together (3 or 4 lines) and then draw another group of vertical lines standing tall. Continue drawing these groups of lines next to each other, one after the other. Repeat drawing the same groups directly below, switching off between horizontal and vertical dashes.*

- *Think of the night sky and create stars that sparkle. To make a star, draw a horizontal line, then a vertical line over it. Next, add two diagonal lines to make an x on top. Repeat and continue drawing more to fill your page. You can even add some dots for the smaller stars and crescent moons.*

- *Using the curved arch shape, draw one after the other starting from the top and going down to the bottom of the page. Then, when you get to the bottom, go back to the top and draw the same shape but upside down. Continue drawing, and you'll start to see a pattern come to life.*

3) If you have other colored pens, experiment with making every other line a different color or use the colors of the rainbow to fill up the entire page. This is your time to dream and play!

4) When you are done drawing, here are a few ideas of where to use your patterns:

- *Cut them into smaller pieces and make a collage. You can layer other photos and tape them to a larger sheet to make a perfect binder cover.*

- *Tape them up to your wall using removable tape.*

- *Turn them into folded cards and write a message on the inside.*

- *Keep them as full sheets and use as wrapping paper to wrap a small present.*

TAKE IT SLOW

It's time for a little pep talk. You'll see some of these sprinkled throughout the book, and it's a space where you and I can check in. I imagine you're reading this and wanting to rush to the end and make all of those projects. Or maybe you're thinking you already know how to write the ABCs so you don't need to go through the beginning lessons.

What I ask of you now is to take it slow. Yes, you might feel confident with some of these lessons already, but did you know that hand lettering is different than handwriting? Hand lettering is drawing letters, and handwriting is what you use to write your homework. This is my

Hand lettering

And this is my

handwriting

Yes, my handwriting is usually scribbles.

These beginning lessons are going to help you see how and why hand lettering is different than handwriting. So, stick with me, and you are going to get really good at this whole hand-lettering thing.

xo, Nicole

LESSON #2

CREATING THE LETTERS

a b c d e f
g h i j k l m
n o p q r s t
u v w x y z

There's a reason why you started this hand-lettering journey with shapes and symbols. The circles, lines, curves, and dots you practiced in Lesson 1 are now going to help you make letters.

Do you see the pink and orange colors in the ABCs above? First, look at the orange lines. Then, look only at the pink lines. Do you see the different shapes? Each letter is a combination or a longer version of each shape and symbol you just practiced.

Try this out: Draw each letter, shape by shape, to create your own alphabet. Instead of just writing an *a*, think of drawing a circle and a line close together. And for *b*, draw a line and either a curve or a circle that overlaps the line. Continue drawing the rest of the letters this way. Feel free to use two colors as I've done here or just one color.

$$O + l = a \qquad l + c = b$$

$$- + c = e \qquad \lceil + - = f$$

$$o + J = g \qquad l + n = h$$

Once you have gone through the lowercase letters, use the same technique to draw the uppercase letters and numbers. You can use the examples on the next page as a guide.

A B C D E F

G H I J K L M

N O P Q R S

T U V W X Y Z

1 2 3 4 5 6 7 8 9 0

Remember what I mentioned in our pep talk on page 17—your hand lettering is different than your handwriting. This is your hand lettering. You are drawing lines and shapes and combining them to form letters. You are well on your way to hand lettering now!

PROJECT #2
HANGING BANNER

Is there a place above your bed that could use some decoration? Or do you have a fun party coming up that you want to make a banner for? Let's take the letters you just practiced and create your own banner to hang up loud and proud!

SUPPLIES:

O **scratch paper**

O **pencil**

O **scissors**

O **cardstock**

O **marker** (I suggest a thicker marker)

O **hole punch**

O **string**

O **removable tape or tacks**

1) Pick a word or a short quote to write on your banner. Maybe choose your name if you plan to hang it above your bed.

2) Place a piece of scratch paper over the triangle or flag template on the next page and trace the outline.

3) Cut your triangle or flag out. This is going to be your stencil that you will use over and over again.

4) Gather multiple sheets of cardstock. You can use one color or use several different color papers—you choose!

• *I suggest picking a lighter color paper for now. If you choose black or really dark-colored paper, you may not be able to see the ink from your markers. Later, in Lesson 11, you'll learn about paint pens, which can write on darker paper. After that lesson, you can come back to this project and make more banners with all sorts of color combinations.*

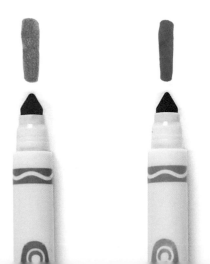

TEMPLATE

TEMPLATE

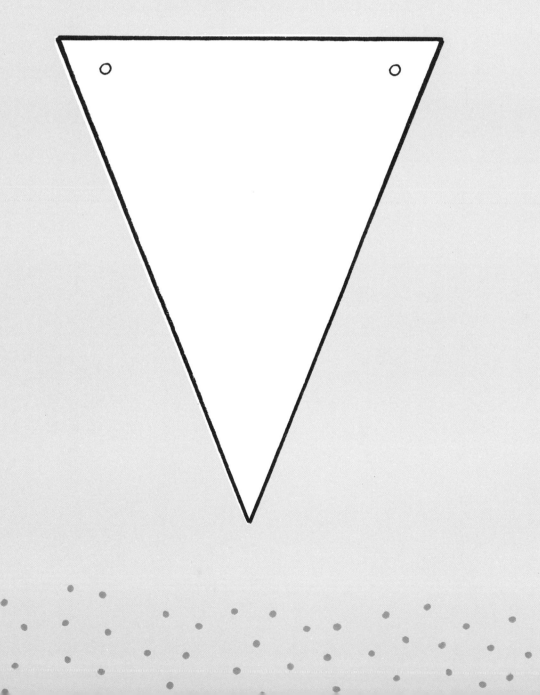

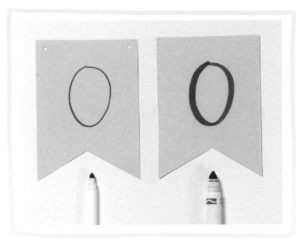

5) Place the stencil you cut out on top of the cardstock and outline the edges of the flag. Then, move the stencil over onto a different blank area of the cardstock and trace another flag. Continue doing this until you have enough flags for each letter in your word. For example, "hello" has 5 letters plus 1 for the sunshine symbol, so I made 6 flags. When you have traced enough flags, cut out each one using scissors.

6) Now, it's time to use your hand-lettering skills. With a pencil, *lightly* draw each letter on its own flag. Combine the shapes like you learned in this lesson to make your letters.

7) With a pen, trace over the pencil lines of each letter you made in Step 6. I suggest using a bigger marker to create a thicker line since your banner will likely be read from farther away. The photo above shows the difference between using a smaller marker (left) and using a bigger marker, like the Crayola Broad Line Markers (right).

8) After you have drawn each letter, you can add a border around the edges of the flags using any of the shapes you learned in Lesson 1. Have fun making your banner unique!

9) With a hole punch, cut out two circles at the top corners of each flag.

26

10) Organize and lay out the flags in order to spell out your word.

11) With string in one hand and your first letter flag in the other, thread the string through the left hole and then through the right hole. Then, pick up the next letter and thread the string through both holes the same way. Continue stringing each letter and watch your banner come to life right before your eyes. Once you thread the string through the last letter, cut the string, leaving a little bit extra on the ends.

12) Use removable tape or thumbtacks and hang each end of the banner on the wall. Ask a friend to hold one side of the banner up while you hang the other side. Finally, step back and look at what you created. Bravo!

Tip

Wrap a piece of tape around the end of the string to prevent the end from fraying as you thread it through each hole. This is similar to the end of a shoelace.

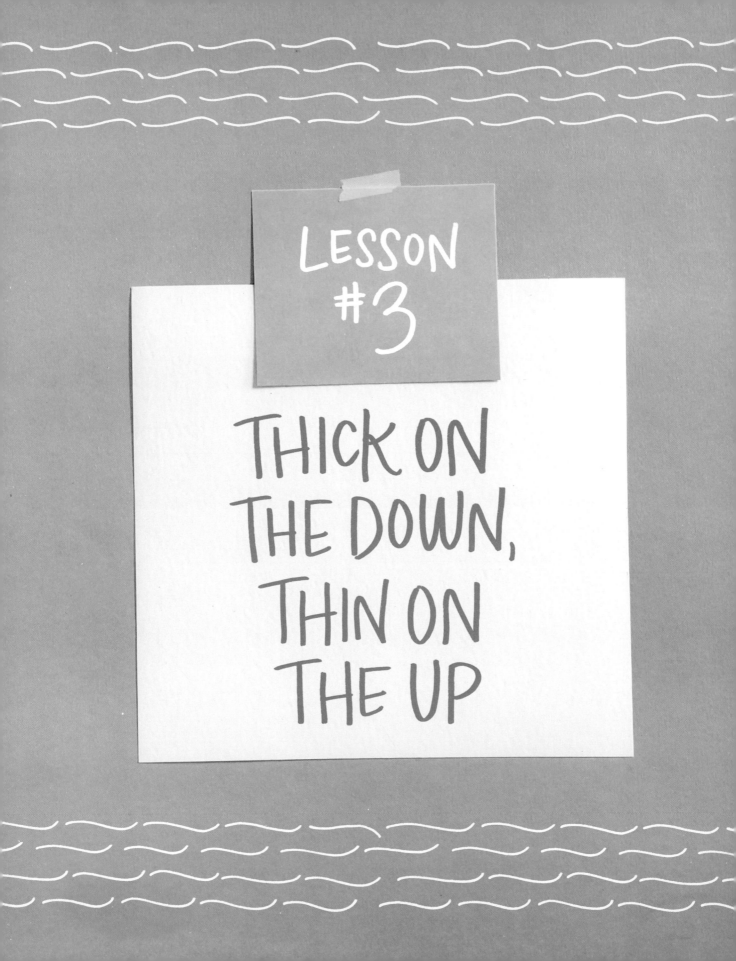

LESSON #3

THICK ON THE DOWN, THIN ON THE UP

Take a look at the three *Januarys* written below. What is different about each of them? They all have the same letters—*j, a, n, u, a, r, y*— but there's something unique about each one. I'll give you a hint: it has to do with line thickness.

January

January

January

The first *January* is drawn with just thin lines; the second *January* is drawn with both thin lines and thick lines; and the third *January* is drawn with just thick lines. Can you see it now?

What you are learning in this lesson is how to make your lettering look like the second *January*, with thin and thick lines. And no, the answer is not the use of a different pen. Say this with me: *thick on the down, thin on the up*. Looking at the arrows on *January* below, you can see that when the arrow is pointing down, the line is thick, and when the arrow is pointing up, the line is thin.

Now that you can see the difference, let's break it down and show you how to write in this style:

1) First, write your word with some space between each letter.

February

2) Then, figure out which lines of your letters need to be thicker. To do this, pretend to draw over your letters, and watch as your fingers move up and down. Remember the saying you just learned: *thick on the down, thin on the up*. When your fingers move downward, that line will need to be thicker. For example, on the straight line of the *F*, the curve of the *e*, and the straight line of the *b*. So, those parts will be the thicker lines. If it helps you to remember, draw the arrows in pencil on your own words first, then erase them later. When your fingers are moving upward or horizontally, you can leave the line as is since it is already thin.

February

3) On the parts you need to make thicker, draw another line right next to it with some space between. Then, connect the lines to create a closed shape.

February → February

On a curved letter like the *e*, draw the same curved shape so it naturally connects back. Connect the lines right away like the example below.

Now, take a look at the *o*'s below. The thick down stroke on the first *o* is created with a straight line, while the second *o* is created with a curved line. The curved line creates a smooth transition and connects back like a crescent moon. This is what you want. Try to avoid making a harsh edge like in the first *o*.

4) Finally, color in the empty space you created (the area between the line you added and the original line) so it looks like one thick stroke. And then that's it! You just completed your word with both thin and thick lines.

February

Now that you know the steps to create this thin and thick style, practice with the rest of the months to complete a full year. Remember to add the thick down stroke when your hand is moving downward. *Thick on the down, thin on the up.*

PROJECT#3
STICKY NOTE CALENDAR

NOVEMBER

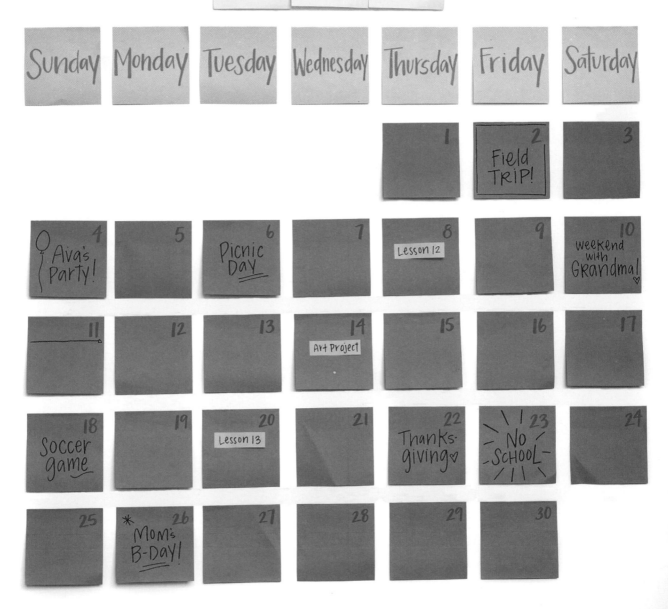

Sunday	Monday	Tuesday	Wednesday	Thursday	Friday	Saturday
				1	2 Field TRIP!	3
4 Ava's Party!	5	6 Picnic Day	7	8 Lesson 12	9	10 Weekend with Grandma!
11	12	13	14 Art Project	15	16	17
18 Soccer game	19	20 Lesson 13	21	22 Thanks-giving	23 NO SCHOOL	24
25	26 Mom's B-DAY!	27	28	29	30	

Do you use a calendar to remember all the fun activities you have planned for the month? If not, this project might be the perfect one for you to get started! You'll know when your friend's birthday party is, the date of your next school field trip, and it can be helpful for your whole family too!

SUPPLIES:

- ○ **sticky notes**

- ○ **scratch paper**

- ○ **pencil**

- ○ **any pen/marker**

- ○ **removable tape** (washi tape recommended)

1) Have you ever seen small pads of paper on your teacher's desk or in your parents' office? Those pieces of paper are called sticky notes or Post-it Notes and usually come in bright yellow, or sometimes even colors like pink or blue. Ask an adult if you can use some for your project. Mention that you will be making a calendar and will show him or her when you are done.

2) On scratch paper, practice drawing the days of the week and add the thick line when your hand is moving down like you just learned.

3) Then, take 7 sticky notes from the pad and use your marker to draw each day of the week on a separate sticky note.

33

Sunday

Monday

Tuesday

Wednesday

Thursday

Friday

Saturday

4) Find out how many days are in this month. There are either 30 or 31 days, except for February, which has 28 (or 29 if it's a leap year). Each day will have its own sticky note and you can pick which corner to draw the number in.

TOP or BOTTOM

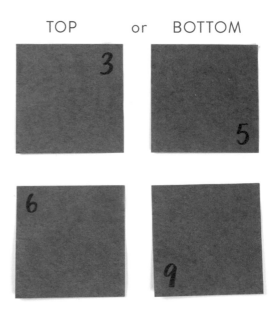

5) Then, for the month, we're going to make it bigger so it stands out. To do this, lay out 3 sticky notes side by side touching one another and pretend you have one long sticky note. Using a pencil, draw your letters bigger by breaking up the word into three parts. For example, when drawing *November*, the first

NOVEMBER

sticky note can have the letters *N*, *O*, and part of the *V*. The second sticky note can have the other part of the *V*, the *E*, *M*, and part of the *B*. The last sticky note has the other part of the *B*, the *E*, and the *R*. Finally, trace over the full word in pen.

6) To put your calendar together, find a blank wall big enough to fit 7 sticky notes across. Then, take a look

at the photo on page 37. Do you see the pink washi tape? That removable tape is the trick to keeping everything straight. Place one long strip of removable tape on the wall. Stick the Sunday sticky note below the tape on the left side. Then, stick the rest of the days, one by one, below the tape in that same row. Keep a little bit of space between each day.

7) After placing the Saturday sticky note on that row, add another long strip of tape right below. Then, find out what day of the week the 1st of the month starts on. Start placing the date sticky notes on that day and go in order. When you get to the end of the week, add another long horizontal strip of tape below and continue adding the rest of the days of the month.

8) Add the month name to the top of your calendar. Place those sticky notes right next to each other, touching, so it looks like one word.

9) Very carefully, remove the tape above and below each row. If a sticky note falls, that's okay. Just pick it up and stick it back to the wall.

10) Your calendar is now ready to be used. Hooray! Do you have any important events coming up? Is there a birthday party or a holiday that you want to mark on your calendar? You can write on another, smaller sticky note to stick onto the dates, or you can write directly on the sticky note itself.

11) Once the month is over, go back to Step 5 and draw the next month. Then, move the numbers around, or if you filled them up you can always make new ones!

TIP

Decorative tape called washi tape can be easily removed from the wall without taking off the paint. Painter's tape (which is typically blue) works great as well.

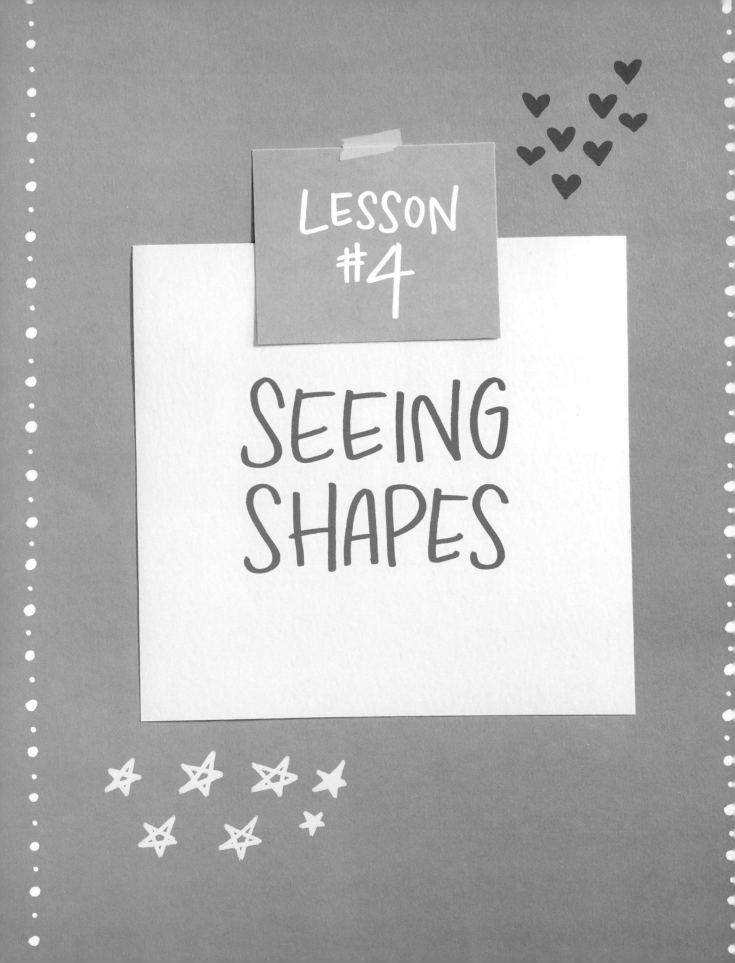

LESSON #4

SEEING SHAPES

What do all of the items in Group 1 have in common that is different than the items in Group 2? Here's a hint—it has to do with this lesson's title.

If you answered that Group 1 has circles instead of ovals or that they are wide instead of skinny, you would be correct! The first group's items are all circular in shape, and the second group's are all oval in shape.

Did you know that your letters can also be thought of as circular or oval? Take a look at the examples below. *Besties* on the left looks different than *Besties* on the right, even though they are the same exact letters. But why? If you look closely at the shapes drawn below each word, you can see that the letters on the left are more circular than the oval letters in *Besties* on the right.

BESTIES   BESTIES

BESTIES   BESTIES

Take a moment to think about your best friend. What words would you use to describe her or him? Is your best friend cool, sweet, awesome, fun, or kind? Write the words describing your friend on the left side of your practice page, each on its own line. Leave some space below each word.

Then, draw the shapes your letters are making, like in the photo below. Are they shaped more like a doughnut and circular, or more like a pineapple and oval? There isn't a right or wrong answer. If your word has a lowercase *l* or *i*, you can skip drawing that shape since those two letters cannot be made into a different shape. A lowercase *t* is similar; however,

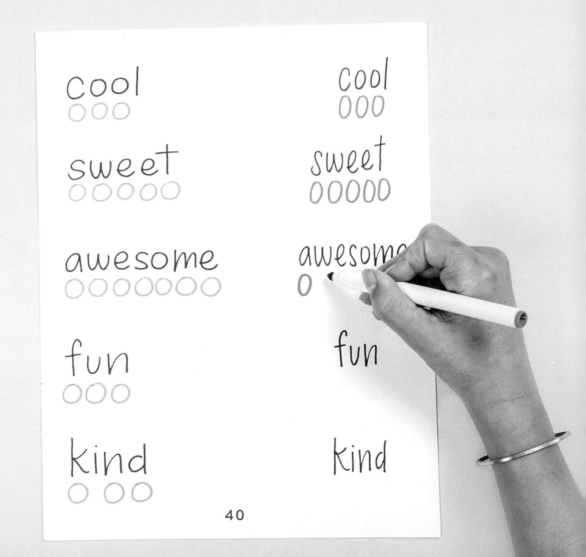

40

you can make the crossing of the *t* longer to be a wider shape, or shorter to be a skinnier shape. This can be seen in *sweet* in the photo.

Once you have the left side of your page filled in, draw the same words on the right side, but with the opposite shape.

❊ If the letters you drew on the left side are more circular, then on the right side of the page, write your letters using oval shapes. To do this, draw the same letters, but think of making them skinnier.

❊ If you started with more oval letters on the left side, then write your letters in a more circular way on the right side. To do this, draw your letters wider to take up more room.

Another way to practice writing in this new style is to draw the circles or ovals first using a pencil. Then, write your letters inside those shapes and take up all of the space, like in the example below. This will help train your mind to draw more wide and circular or skinnier and oval.

OOOOO   OOOOOOOO

DONUT   PINEAPPLE

Remember at the beginning of the book how I said that hand lettering is more than just your handwriting? This is one of the reasons why. Can you see how you just turned your hand lettering into a new style by changing the shapes of your letters? I am confident that it looks different than your handwriting. Great job!

41

PROJECT #4
STICKERS

Hi

GOOD VIBES

YOU'RE COOL

sweet heart

CRAYOLA SUPER TIP MARKER

LEPEN

GELLY ROLL

GELLY ROLL

It's time to apply these new skills to a project and create one-of-a-kind stickers. You can use them to decorate your binder, add them to notes to your friends, or seal the back of an envelope with a hand-lettered thank-you sticker. Have some fun making your very own!

SUPPLIES:

O blank stickers

O scratch paper

O pen/marker

O gel pens

1) There are many types of stickers: circle stickers and oval stickers, big stickers and small stickers. Some have borders on them and some come in different colors. Browse a craft store, check out an office supply store, or find blank sticker sheets online. You can also make your own stickers by using cardstock and adding double-sided tape to the back.

2) Think about the words you want to write on your stickers. Some ideas of phrases are *good vibes*, *super star*, and *dream big*. Or you also have the words from this lesson you used to describe your best friend. Those will make great stickers!

3) Practice first by drawing the shape of your stickers on scratch paper. Then, try using different lettering styles, like the circular and oval styles you learned in this lesson.

Here's an example: Let's say you're writing the phrase *you're awesome* on a circular sticker. You decide to write *you're* with circular letters, but when you draw *awesome* with the same circular style, it won't fit. That's okay! I have a little secret for you: your letters don't all have to be the same shape. You can keep *you're* with circular shapes and then draw *awesome* with oval shapes. This way, the longer word will fit on the sticker.

4) Next, experiment with your pens on scratch paper. The markers you've been using will work great, but if the tip is too big, it might be hard to read on a small sticker. Flip back to page 42 to see a comparison of a few other options.

- *Gel pens: They come in many bright colors, including white and metallic, so you can write on darker paper. My favorite brand of gel pen is Gelly Roll.*

- *Smaller-tipped pen: The brand LePen is really great and also has pens in many colors.*

CIRCULAR SHAPES

CIRCULAR + OVAL SHAPES

5) Now you are ready for your final stickers. Using your practice sheet as reference, draw your words onto the stickers using the marker or pen you like best. Then, add the thick down stroke like you learned in Lesson 3 to make your lettering pop.

6) If you want to add more to your stickers, draw a border or fill the empty space with polka dots. Experiment with different colors and different pens.

7) Finally, peel your hand-lettered stickers and stick away. You can decorate your school binder and add some of the patterns from Project 1, like in the photo here. Make sure to have some stickers for your BFF, too!

LESSON #5

TALL +
NARROW

Each year, you grow taller—or if you're like me, you stay short and are proud of it! But did you know that your letters can also be designed by height? Take a look at the ABCs below. Row 1 is short, Row 2 is a little taller, and Row 3 is the tallest. The ABCs in each row are the same width, but by drawing the letters at different heights, each row has a different look.

Try this out on your own. Take out scratch paper and place it over the grid lines on page 48. Then, fill in the grid and draw your own ABCs with different heights.

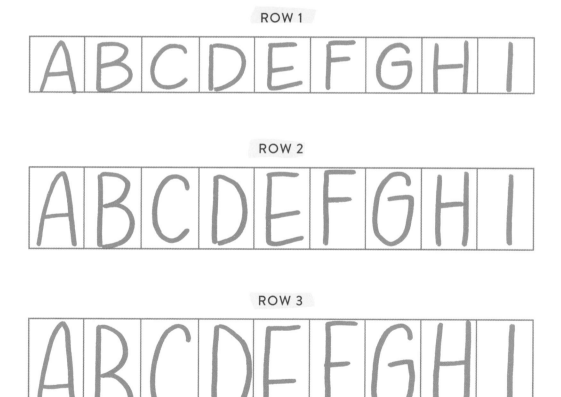

ROW 1

ABCDEFGHI

ROW 2

ABCDEFGHI

ROW 3

ABCDEFGHI

HEIGHT 1

HEIGHT 2

HEIGHT 3

Once you are done with that, try writing your name without the grid. Write it three times, making the letters taller and taller each time. Remember that it's not about making the letters wider, but taller!

Chloe Chloe Chloe

Ethan Ethan Ethan

Next, write your name three more times, but for these ones, instead of making all of the letters taller, only change the height of the lowercase letters. Keep the capital letter of your name the same height in all three versions, like in the examples of *Olivia* below. For the final and tallest one, all of the letters—including the capital letter—will be the same height.

Olivia Olivia Olivia

Finally, take a step back and look at all of your options. These are different lettering styles you can use, and all you did was change the height of your letters!

PROJECT #5
WATERCOLOR BOOKMARK

Even if reading isn't your favorite subject, you can make a bookmark to use in your school notebook. A bookmark is simply there to help you mark your spot, and it's even better if it's a pretty one that you made. They also make great gifts because everyone can use a bookmark for something!

SUPPLIES:

O watercolors

O cup for water

O paper towels

O wide paint brush

O watercolor paper

O scratch paper

O palette

O pen/marker

O scissors

O hole punch (optional)

O string (optional)

1) This project introduces something fun to play with—watercolors!

Watercolor is a type of paint you can use to make pretty background washes. Here are some things to remember before you get started:

- *There are two types of watercolors: ones that come in a tube and dry watercolors in a pan set. Whichever type you have or want to use is just fine.*

- *Have a small jar or cup of water next to you. Paper towels will also come in handy.*

- *You'll be painting a large area, so find a wide brush similar to the one in the photos.*

- *Finally, you'll need both watercolor paper and scratch paper. The scratch paper will go underneath the watercolor paper so the tabletop stays nice and clean.*

2) If you have tube watercolors, squeeze a little bit of the paint out onto a palette first. Then, dip your brush in water and mix it into the watercolor paint.

If your colors are dry, similar to the palette in the photo below, add more water than you would use with the tube watercolors to mix up the color. Think of it as waking up the paint.

3) Now, let's play! Take out a sheet of watercolor paper and try any of these painting techniques to make a watercolor wash. You will be cutting out the bookmark later on, so feel free to use a big sheet.

- **Technique #1:** *Paint in a sweeping back-and-forth motion until it fills the entire paper.*

- **Technique #2:** *Using the flat side of the brush, paint and move your hand in circular motions.*

- **Technique #3:** *Start with just water. First, clean off your brush and make sure it doesn't have any paint on it. Then, dip it in water, and with only water on the brush, paint over the paper. You will not see anything yet. Now, go to your color palette and gather some color. Then, place the tip of your brush directly on the paper and watch the color move along the water.*

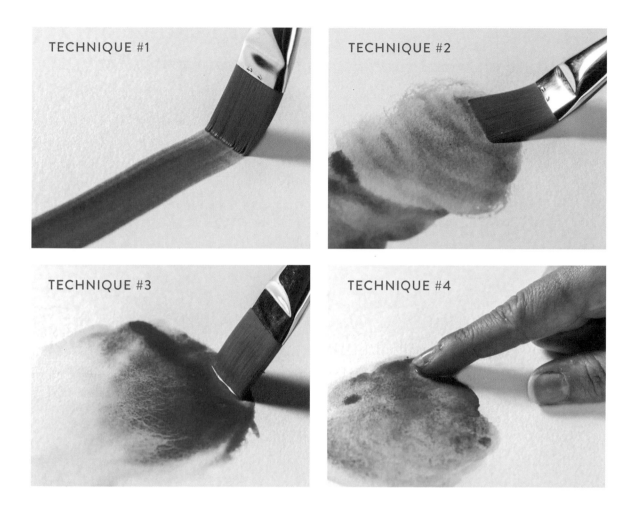

- **Technique #4:** *You don't need a brush for this technique. Wet your fingertip with water and dip it in the paint to pick up some color. Then, on the paper, move your finger in circular motions and cover the surface. This is one of my favorite techniques.*

After you've painted your watercolor washes, wait for the paper to completely dry. It may take a few hours, but it will be worth the wait. Once the paper is dry, if the edges are curling up or down, place a stack of books on top to flatten and reshape. I like to do this overnight and then finish the project in the morning.

4) While you wait for your watercolor paper to dry, flip to page 57 and pick a bookmark size. Then, use scratch paper and trace a few of the bookmark shapes to fill up the page. This will be your practice paper.

5) Choose a quote and practice drawing your design inside the outlined book-mark shapes. Play with how tall or short your letters need to be to fit inside.

For example, looking at the two designs of *Never Give Up,* you can see that the design on the right fills out the bookmark more than the design on the left does. This is because *GIVE* and *UP* are written taller to fill in the space. This is what we're going for.

Now, take a look at the other examples. On the left, the letters in the words *love*, *little*, and *things* are all about the same height, but *THE* is taller to fill in the space. The shorter your word is, the taller your letters can be. You can also see this happening with *LET* and *THE* in the example on the right.

Now, if any of your words are longer, like *ADVENTURE*, those letters will need to be shorter in height and skinnier to fit the space. Another option is to write your phrase horizontally on the bookmark instead of vertically.

6) Once you have your design finalized on your practice paper, cut out one of the bookmark shapes to use as your stencil.

7) Take out the watercolor sheet you painted in Step 3 with the watercolor wash. Place the stencil from Step 6 on top of the paper and outline the rectangle shape in pencil. If you have a big sheet of paper, you can outline more than one to make several bookmarks. Then, cut them out.

8) You're now ready to hand letter your final bookmark. You can use a pencil to lightly draw your phrase first, or just use a marker to write directly on the bookmark. Use your practice sheet for reference.

9) If you're feeling fancy, flip your bookmark over and add a pattern to the back.

10) Finally, use a hole punch to cut a hole at the top of the bookmark. Thread some string through the hole and tie a knot. This way, you can always find your bookmark within the pages of your book. If you cut out a few bookmarks, go ahead and finish the rest, then give them as gifts to your friends or family!

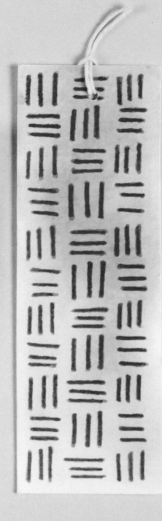

TEMPLATES

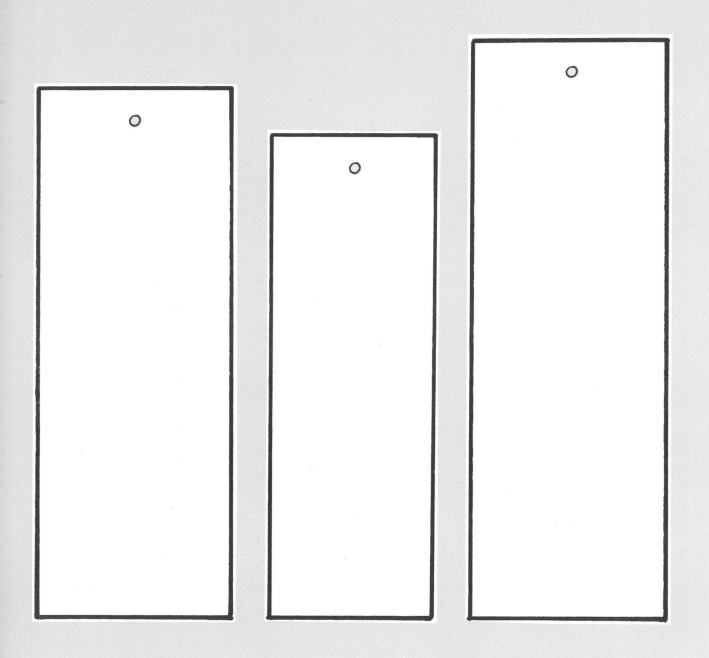

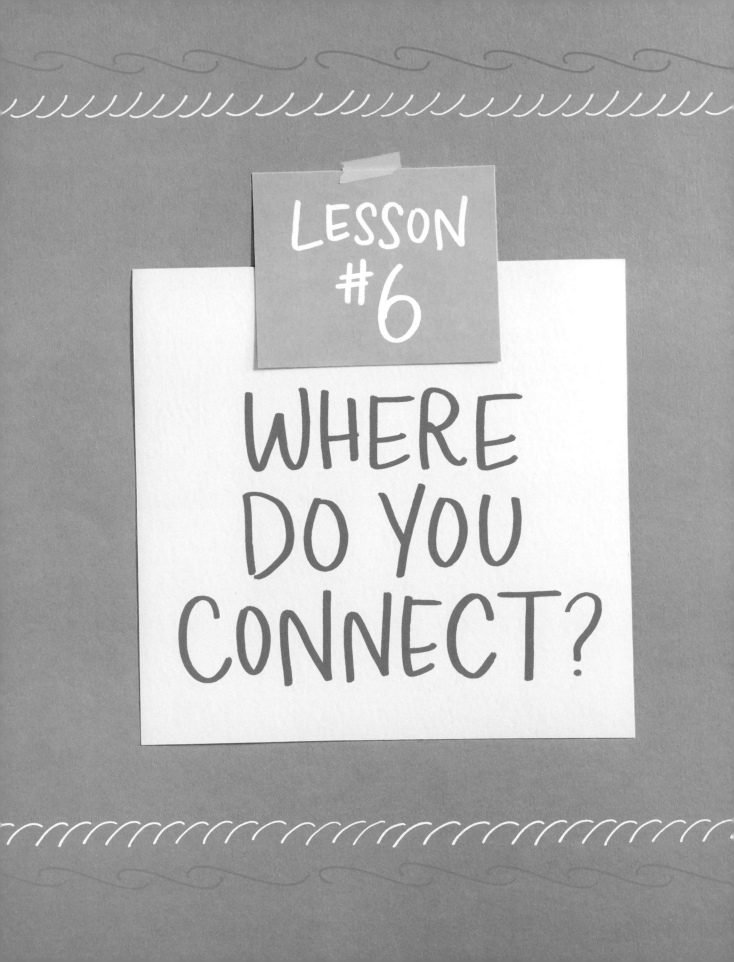

LESSON #6

WHERE DO YOU CONNECT?

Are you starting to see that you can make your hand lettering look different by changing just a few things, like the shape (Lesson 4) and height (Lesson 5) of your letters? You don't need to change a lot to create a whole new look. In this lesson, you'll learn how to add a few new styles to your hand-lettering toolbox.

Look at the three examples below and notice how they are all similar and yet different from one another. Why is that? It's not the shapes nor the height of the letters. The differences between these are a little less obvious.

HAPPY BIRTHDAY

HAPPY BIRTHDAY

HAPPY BIRTHDAY

Before I tell you the answer, I'd like you to draw a capital *H*. Which of the *H*'s below does yours look like?

Now, write another *H*, but draw the horizontal line higher or lower than you did before. It looks different from your first *H*, right? By changing where you draw the horizontal line, you have a new way to write the letter.

This technique also applies to other letters that don't have a horizontal line. For example, the *B*'s below all look different because of where the lines are connected. On the first *B* the top hump ends toward the top. On the second *B*, it ends in the middle. On the third *B* it ends near the bottom.

Now you have the answer to why the *Happy Birthday*'s from the beginning of this lesson look different from one another. You must look at *where* the lines are connected to each other. If you flip back to page 59, can you see how the lines are all drawn at different heights—high on the first example, in the middle on the second example, and low on the last example?

Try this out by writing your own name three different times with all capital letters. First, connect your lines high, then connect your lines in the middle, and finally connect your lines low.

After that, write your name three more times, but this round write with lowercase letters. You may notice that it is less obvious how to change the place where your lines connect. Take a close look at the lowercase *r*, *a*, and *n* in the examples of *Ariana* below.

ARIANA   Ariana

ARIANA   Ariana

ARIANA   Ariana

On the *a*, you can end the curve high, in the middle, or low. And on the *r* and *n*, you can start the second line high, in the middle, or low. They each have a different look, and this is what I want you to experiment with. Now, write your last name and experiment changing where you connect your lines.

a← a← a←   →r →r →r

There are so many different kinds of desserts—cake, cupcakes, chocolates, doughnuts. Do you have a favorite type of dessert? Even if you don't have a birthday coming up, you can always add some fun to your yummy treats with these creative dessert toppers!

SUPPLIES:

O scratch paper

O pencil

O scissors

O cardstock

O pen/marker/gel pen

O double-sided tape

O wooden sticks

O tape

1) First, decide what words to add to your dessert topper. Some ideas are *Wahoo!*, *Yay!*, or *Yippee!*

2) Practice your word on scratch paper and think about the different ways you can change where you connect your lines: high, low, or in the middle. You are the designer, and hand lettering is about expressing your unique self. So, there is no right or wrong way to do this.

3) On page 64, you'll see different options for toppers you can make. Take another piece of scratch paper and place it on top of the templates. Trace over the one you want to make and then cut it out. This is your stencil.

4) Then, grab your cardstock for the final toppers and place your stencil from Step 3 on top. Outline the shape and if you have more room on your cardstock, go ahead and outline more toppers.

63

5) Draw your design:

TEMPLATES 1 AND 2:
Using a marker or gel pen, write your word on both sides of the dotted line to make a front and a back to your toppers. Then, cut them out.

TEMPLATE 3:
If you have a longer phrase, like *Happy Birthday*, you can make a banner for each word and have a taller dessert topper like that shown in the photo on page 66. Then, cut them out.

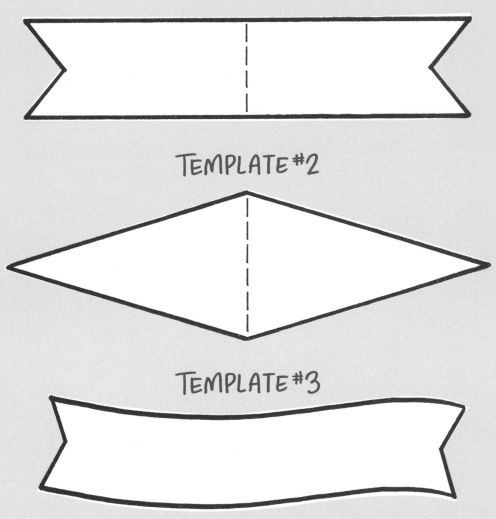

TEMPLATE #1

TEMPLATE #2

TEMPLATE #3

6) Complete the dessert toppers:

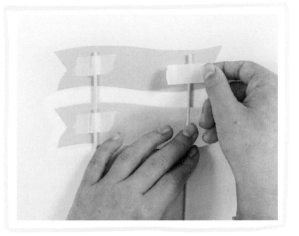

TEMPLATES 1 AND 2:

Flip the topper over and add double-sided tape to the back. Use one long strip of tape that covers the full topper and add any additional smaller pieces if needed so the edges stick together.

    Place a stick at the center of the double-sided tape and fold the topper in half. You should see your word on both the front and the back. If your sticks are too long, bend and cut them. You could also use toothpicks if your desserts are small.

TEMPLATE 3:

Flip the banners over to the back and lay them one above the other in the order of how they will be read. Place the sticks on the right and left sides of the banners. Add regular tape over each stick to secure them to the cardstock. If your sticks are too long, bend and cut them.

7) Finally, poke the sticks inside the desserts, and now you have fun dessert toppers to enjoy!

TRY SOMETHING NEW

Hey, I see you over there working hard to learn something new. I love it. And I can also understand if you are getting a little frustrated *because* you are learning something new. I love that, too. Frustration means you are challenging yourself and pushing yourself out of your comfort zone. And a lot of people don't do that (even for adults this can sometimes be hard).

But you know what is so cool? You are giving something new a try. And no one can ever really judge you for that, because no matter what, you are using your own two hands, being creative, and expressing yourself through hand lettering. Keep going and continue challenging yourself to try new things, both with hand lettering and with your life!

xo, Nicole

LESSON
#7

BRUSH
PENS

Remember how in the beginning of this book I told you that you can do hand lettering with any type of pen? I hope you've been experimenting and have seen that this is true. Well, guess what? I have another great pen type for you to try out and it's called a brush pen. Brush pens have a flexible tip, which means if you press down and draw, the tip will also bend, just like a brush does. There are many brands available, and a few of my favorites are Tombow Dual Brush Pens and the Pentel Fude Touch Sign Pen.

Take out practice paper and experiment. Draw a few lines with your brush pen and play with how hard you push the tip on the paper.

Did you notice that if you press lightly, the line will be thinner? And if you press harder, your line will be thicker? This is because the tip of a brush pen is flexible and bends, which makes a thicker line. The examples below show the range of lines that a Tombow Dual Brush Pen can make.

LIGHT PRESSURE

MEDIUM PRESSURE

HEAVY PRESSURE

There are two parts of the brush pen you will be using: the *tip* and the *belly*. Use the tip to make a thin stroke and the belly to make a thicker stroke. Take out another piece of practice paper and trace over the ABCs on page 71. You will notice these letters have both thin and thick lines, so practice using the tip and the belly of the brush pen here.

Once you have tried that, let's refresh your memory. In Lesson 3, you learned about *thick on the down, thin on the up*. Feel free to flip back to page 29 to review. When you are drawing with a brush pen, instead of adding the thick down stroke *afterward* like you would with a regular marker, you will now create the thick down stroke *while* you draw the letter, by applying heavy pressure.

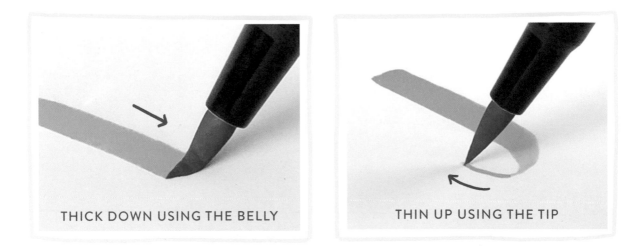

THICK DOWN USING THE BELLY

THIN UP USING THE TIP

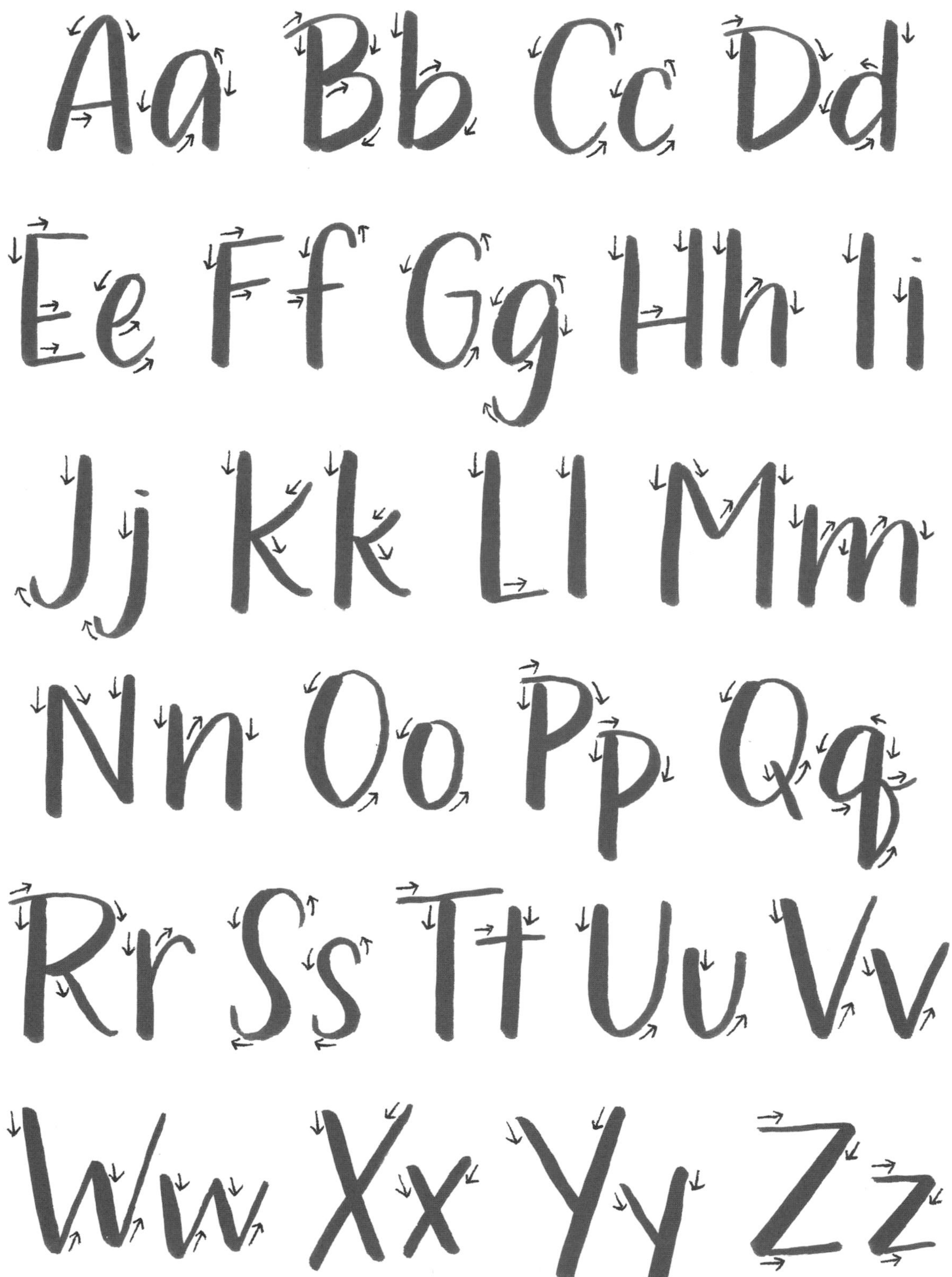

Aa Bb Cc Dd

Ee Ff Gg Hh Ii

Jj Kk Ll Mm

Nn Oo Pp Qq

Rr Ss Tt Uu Vv

Ww Xx Yy Zz

Now, use your brush pen and draw your ABCs slowly, focusing on drawing them stroke by stroke. Remember the shapes you learned in Lesson 1? Combine them to make the letters. For example, an uppercase *B* has three lines, as shown in the example below. Draw your *B* again, and this time take it slower and follow these instructions:

1) Draw the straight line down first using medium to heavy pressure, then stop.

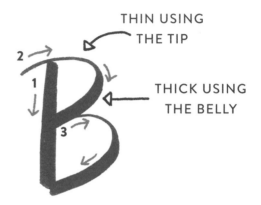

THIN USING THE TIP

THICK USING THE BELLY

2) For the curved line, remember to use the tip of the brush pen to start the line. As you round the curve, start to press harder for the thick down stroke. Do not lift up your hand—just apply more pressure.

3) Finally, for the last curved line, do the same thing. Start by lightly grazing the paper using the tip of the brush pen. Then, use the belly of the brush as you round the curve.

Continue to practice with your brush pen. It can be a little tricky in the beginning since these pens act differently than other tools. If you find yourself getting frustrated, flip back to page 67 for the pep talk. Challenge yourself to try something new, and you may start to love this new pen!

PROJECT #7
PARTY HATS

Time to celebrate! You just learned a new pen to add to your toolbox, and that deserves a party. Invite your friends over to make some party hats and teach them your new hand-lettering skills!

SUPPLIES:

O scratch paper

O pencil

O scissors

O cardstock

O cardboard box

O ballpoint pen

O brush pen/marker

O tape

O string/ribbon/elastic

1) First, make your stencil. Trace over the party-hat template on page 75 using scratch paper. Add the two x marks as well. Then, cut out your stencil.

2) Choose the colored cardstock that you want to make your hats out of. You can pick one or a variety of colors.

3) Place the stencil from Step 1 on top of your cardstock and outline the party-hat shape. Then, cut them out.

4) Ask an adult if they have two things: a sturdy cardboard box that will eventually be thrown away and a ballpoint pen. These will help you make the holes in your hats. Place the hat flat on the cardboard box and poke the point of the ballpoint pen through one of the x marks. The goal is to poke through the cardstock to make a hole. Do the same thing on the other x mark.

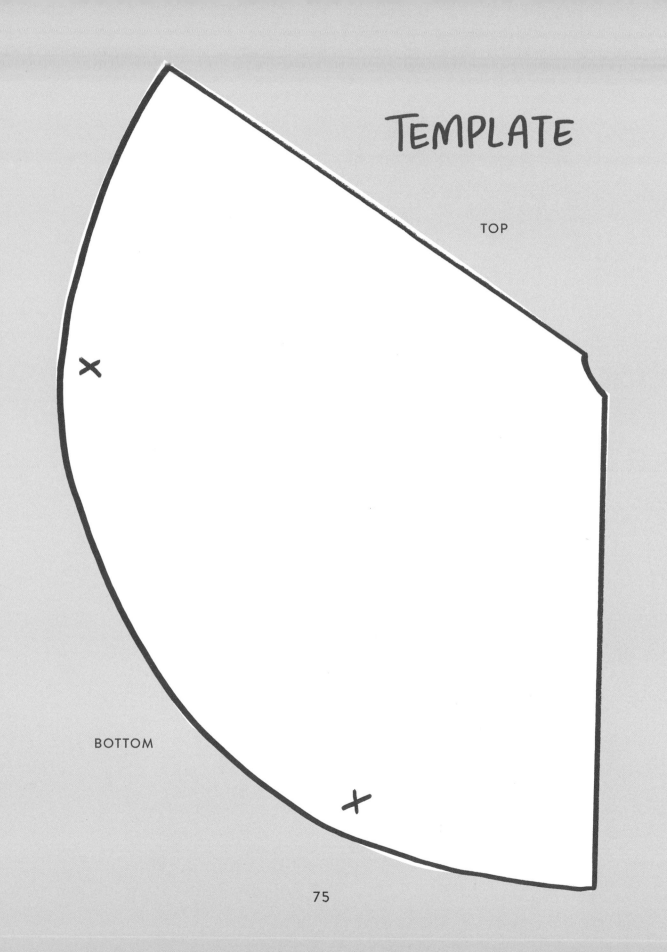

TEMPLATE

TOP

X

BOTTOM

X

75

5) Time to design. The pointed part is the top of the hat, and the wide part is the bottom. Draw your design using a brush pen like you learned in this lesson. If you do not have a brush pen, you can still complete this project by using any marker you have in your toolbox. Here are a few ideas for your design:

- *Pick a fun phrase and repeat it to make a pattern, like I did with the phrase* hip hip hooray.

- *Write your name in the center. Then, add patterns around it to fill the rest of the space.*

- *Make a full party hat with just patterns.*

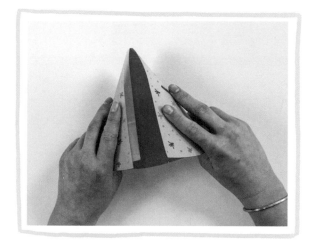

6) Before taping your hat together, form the paper into a cone shape using your hand. This helps mold the paper without creasing it.

7) Then, with your design facing up, add a long strip of tape to the right side so it hangs over the edge, like in the photo above. The sticky part of the tape will be facing down.

8) Fold the hat to create a cone shape and overlap the edges slightly, like in the second photo above. It helps to focus on the pointed part first and then press the tape down. After, add more tape on the outside and inside over the overlapping seam so the edges stay together.

9) Grab string, ribbon, or elastic and thread it through one of the holes from the outside in and tie a knot. If the knot is too small, make another one on top of that knot to make a larger knot. Place the hat back on your head and ask a friend to help you measure how much string you need. Wrap the string under your chin, and add a little extra. Cut to that length and thread it through the other hole, again from the outside in. Tie a knot so the string is tight enough that the hat will stay on your head, but not too tight.

10) Finally, make the rest of the hats, and then it's time to celebrate! Hip hip hooray!

LESSON #8

PLAYING WITH ANGLES

To begin, take out any practice papers that already have your hand lettering on them. This can be designs from this book or any practice lettering you've done separately. Looking at your own words, do any of your letters look like they are leaning to one side or the other? Or do all your letters stand up straight?

To figure out the angles of your own letters, set your pen down on the table and lay it over your words. Move the pen across each letter to match the horizontal lines you drew. Notice if your pen is straight or angled from letter to letter.

For example, in the word *shine* below, all of the letters are standing up straight.

Now, compare the first *shine* to the second one below. Can you see the difference? All of these letters look like they are leaning over. This is the angled hand-lettering style.

Now, you can see that changing the position of the lines and strokes can create a whole new style to add to your hand-lettering toolbox.

I have something that will help you write your letters at an angle—the angled grid lines on the next page. To use this guide, place your practice paper on top so you can see the lines through the page. Then, follow the angled lines as you draw your letters. Each line does not need to be perfectly drawn over the angled lines, but rather just parallel to it. For example, the word *bright* on the left follows the angled grid lines while *bright* on the right doesn't. Can you see the difference?

BRIGHT BRIGHT

Now you can add drawing at an angle to your hand-lettering toolbox! Continue practicing and try different words.

DREAM

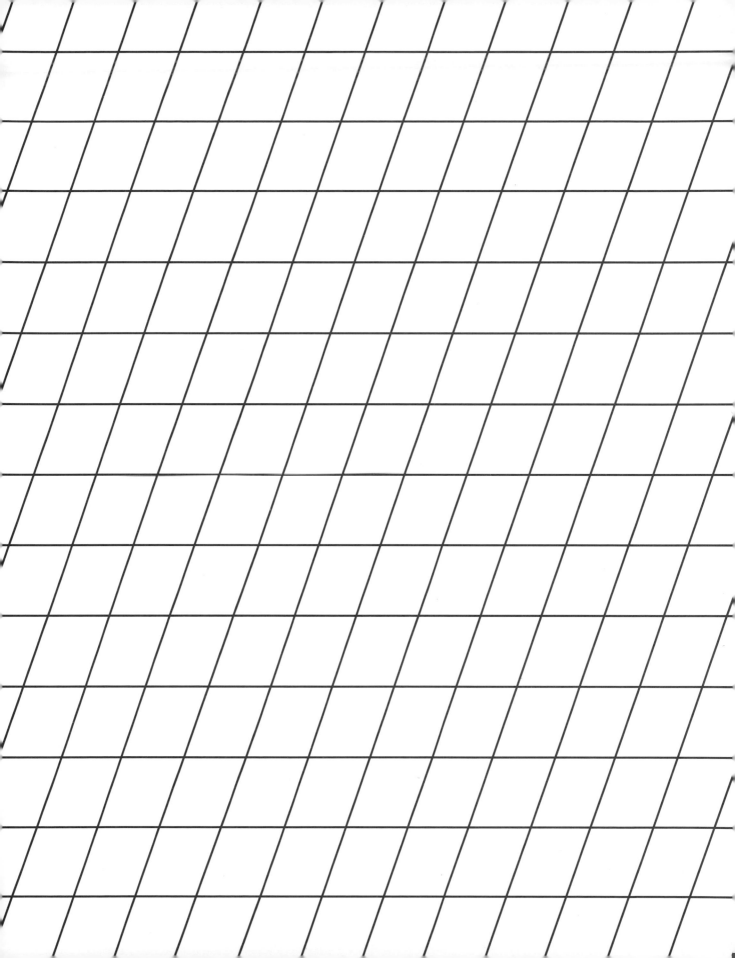

Now that you know a new lettering style, let's apply your skills and make wall art to decorate your room, your locker, or any other place where you can show off some of your personality.

SUPPLIES:

O   picture frame (optional)

O   scratch paper

O   pencil

O   cardstock

O   removable tape

O   scissors

O   dark marker

O   marker or brush pen

1) Do you have a favorite saying or an inspirational quote that makes you happy? A few of my favorites are: *Have Courage, Be Brave,* or *Shine Bright.* Pick one that you want to draw.

2) If you plan to frame your wall art, figure out how big the picture frame you want to use is. Some standard sizes are 4 x 6 inches, 5 x 7 inches, or 8 x 10 inches.

Here's a shortcut: take the paper out of your picture frame and use that as your template. Outline the outside of this shape on scratch paper to use as your practice paper. Then, outline the same shape on your final cardstock so you know that it will fit in the frame perfectly when you are done.

3) For the design, decide if you want your letters to be slanted or standing straight. If you'd like them to be slanted, remember you have the angled grid on page 81 to help you out if needed. Place your scratch paper on top of the angled grid and draw out your letters in pencil first. This will be your stencil.

4) When you have your design figured out, trace over your pencil lines in a dark marker. It will make sense why in a few steps. This is not your final art piece yet.

5) Now, you may be thinking, "*How do I get that same design from my practice paper onto my final cardstock?*" Good question. I have a little secret for you. It's called a window! The next time the sun is shining through a window in your home or room, tape the stencil you made in Step 4 to the window. Use removable tape so it can be easily removed once you're done.

6) Cut out your final cardstock from Step 2 and tape it on the window over your stencil. Match up the rectangle shape like in the photo above on the right. You will be able to see your quote through the paper. It's like magic!

If you can't see the words through your cardstock, your cardstock may be too thick or too dark colored. Unfortunately, this magic trick doesn't work with darker paper. If you have a lighter colored cardstock, use that instead.

7) Now all you need to do is trace the lettering. Use a marker or brush pen (Lesson 7) and trace your design.

8) Add any patterns to add some fun to your art and fill up the space.

9) Once you're done, place your art inside a frame and hang it up loud and proud!

STRAIGHT
HAND-LETTERING
STYLE

ANGLED
HAND-LETTERING
STYLE

LESSON
#9

THE
SPACE
BETWEEN

Let's talk about space. No, not outer space, though that's a pretty cool topic! I'm talking about the space between letters.

NOTEBOOK

Take a look at *notebook* above. Something doesn't feel right about this word. But why? I'll give you a hint: it has to do with the space between each letter.

Even though *notebook* is one full word, *note* and *book* look like two separate parts. The reason for that is because the empty spaces between the letters are different sizes. I drew colored shapes on the example below to show you. The shapes between the letters in *note* are wide circles (pink), while the shapes between *book*'s letters are skinnier ovals (orange). We learned about the shapes of letters in Lesson 4, but now we're looking at the shapes of the empty spaces *between* the letters.

NOTEBOOK

Now that you are aware of the spaces between the letters, did you know that you can create another style of hand lettering simply by making the space between your letters bigger or smaller? You can draw your word with wide circles, like the first *notebook* below, or with skinny ovals, like the second *notebook* below.

NOTEBOOK
NOTEBOOK

Try this out on your own, starting with your name. Write it once with small spaces between each letter. Then, draw it again, but this time leave more room between each letter. If it helps to practice, draw the shapes in pencil between each letter and then erase them afterward. By simply changing the space between the letters, you now have more ways to make your hand lettering look different.

PROJECT#9
NOTEBOOK

Do you have a journal or a notebook where you keep your biggest dreams, the places you want to visit, or memories with your friends? If you don't have one, you will soon enough! This notebook will be your place to write down all your thoughts, dreams, and top-secret secrets.

SUPPLIES:

O 3+ sheets of computer paper

O 1 sheet of cardstock

O pencil

O scratch paper

O marker/brush pen

O hole punch

O string

1) Take out a few pieces of computer paper along with one piece of cardstock for the notebook's cover. Place the cardstock on the table first, then put the computer papers on top of that.

2) Fold all of the papers in half, with the cardstock on the outside. This will create a 5.5 x 8.5-inch booklet.

3) Trace the outline of the cover on scratch paper and practice drawing your design. You can write your name and the word *notebook,* just as you did in the lesson exercise. Simply add an apostrophe and an *s* to the end of your name and then add the year below. Now you have your design all set!

4) Take the cover cardstock off the booklet you folded in Step 2 and open it up. You'll want to write on the right outside part of the folded paper so the cover is in the right spot when you put the booklet back together. Have your practice paper next to you as you copy your lettering design. Add other patterns around your words to decorate the cover.

5) Once you're done drawing, add the cover back to the outside of the computer sheets and open the notebook.

6) Add two hole punches on the fold— one about an inch from the top and the other the same distance from the bottom. If the paper is too thick, hole-punch the computer papers by themselves first and then the cardstock on its own.

7) Finally, grab some string and thread it through both holes. If your string is thin, you can thread it a few times to make sure the papers are secure. Tie a knot on the inside, and you now have your very own notebook!

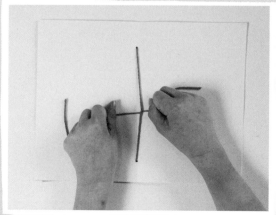

LESSON #10

EXPLORING YOUR STYLE

— PART 1 —

Look at you go! You made it to Lesson 10, and now you have so many hand-lettering styles to use for new projects. Let's review a few of them:

LESSON 9

SKINNY SPACE STYLE

Hello

WIDE SPACE STYLE

Hello

LESSON 8

STANDING STRAIGHT STYLE

Hello

SLANTED ANGLE STYLE

Hello

LESSON 4

CIRCULAR STYLE

Hello

OVAL STYLE

Hello

Individually, those are all great styles of hand lettering for you to use. But what if you were to combine them?

On the next page, the word *beautiful* is written three different ways. Looking at the scales to the right of each word, you'll see the three styles we just talked about—*spacing*, *angle*, and *shape*. The icons below each one show you the range of options to experiment with. The spacing can go from tight (ABC) to wide (A B C); the angle can go from straight (|||) to slanted (///); and the shape can go from circular (OOO) to oval (000).

The heart on each line shows you where on the scale the word *beautiful* is written. For example, the first *beautiful* has wide spacing, slanted angles, and oval-shaped letters. The second *beautiful* has medium spacing, straight angles, and circular-shaped letters. The third *beautiful* has tight spacing, straight angles, and oval-shaped letters. Cool, right?

Try this out on your own: first copy and make the same scale. Then, add a heart somewhere along each line for *spacing*, *angle*, and *shape*. Say to yourself, *The spacing is _____ (fill in), the angle is _____ (fill in), and the shape is _____ (fill in), so I need to draw my letters following those as my guides.* After you do it once, try it again, but change the placement of one of the hearts along the scale. Try this out as many times as you want. You'll start to see new styles of hand lettering come to life, all with the same word!

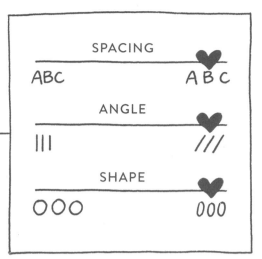

beautiful —

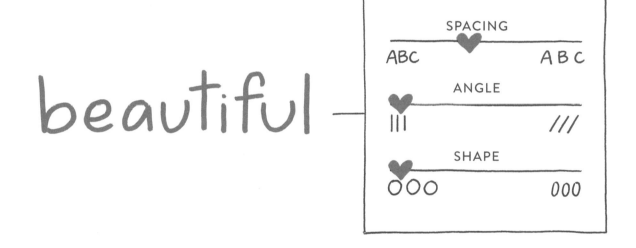

beautiful —

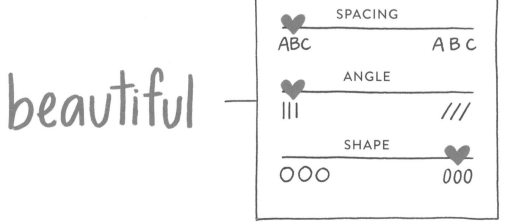

beautiful —

PROJECT #10
PLACEMATS

Avery

Aiden

Dani ♡

Now that you have more hand-lettering styles to choose from, let's get some practice in by making placemats. Surprise your parents with their very own personalized placemats at your next family dinner. They'll be super impressed with your hand-lettering skills!

SUPPLIES:

O large cardstock or watercolor paper

O scratch paper

O pencil

O markers/brush pens

1) To start, try to find paper that is bigger than standard notebook or computer paper. Some craft stores sell cardstock in sheets that are 12 x 12 inches or watercolor paper that is 12 x 18 inches. If you can't find bigger paper, that's okay. You can also buy poster board and cut it down to the size you would like. Placemats can be square, rectangular, circular, or oval— you get to choose which you like best.

2) Practice writing the names on scratch paper. Challenge yourself to use a different hand-lettering style for each person. Remember: You can use the scales you just learned in this lesson.

3) Take out your placemat paper from Step 1 and decide where to write the name. Do you want it written to the right or to the left? Or maybe in the middle on a curve? Put a plate on the placemat first so you can imagine where the name should go. Then, draw a light pencil line on that spot to use as your guideline.

4) Remove the plate and have your practice paper with names from Step 2 next to you. You can either write the name in pencil first or go for it and draw with your lettering tool.

5) Add the thick down strokes you learned in Lesson 3 to make your letters bolder. Or, if you are using a brush pen, draw your letters with the thin and thick lines by using the tip and belly like you learned in Lesson 7.

6) Fill in the space around the plate with patterns to add some personality to the placemats, or draw a border around the edges.

Another fun trick is to use multiple colors to create a gradient pattern like the photo on page 99. To do this, start with the shapes on the left side using one color. Draw a few more shapes from the pattern to overlap into the middle section. Then, choose a different color and continue drawing the pattern in the middle of the placemat. Remember to overlap into the next section to create a smooth transition. Finally, choose a third color to draw the rest of the pattern on the right side. Now you have a fun and colorful ombre placemat!

7) Finally, set the placemats out on the table, add plates and silverware, and watch everyone smile when they see their name on their very own placemat. Bravo!

Kaleigh

LESSON
#11

PAINT
PENS

Let's switch gears and talk a little more about lettering tools. You've learned about markers, gel pens, and brush pens, and there are plenty of other great pens yet to be explored!

Have you ever wondered how to write on different surfaces, like glass, wood, or even leaves? If you've tried to use markers on those surfaces before, you might have found that the color doesn't stay and spreads out.

Enter paint pens. This is a new pen to add to your toolbox. There are many brands out there, and a few I recommend are Sharpie Paint Markers, Molotow, and Sakura Pen-touch Paint Markers.

TIP

The next time you try to write on a surface and the marker is just not working, try using a paint pen. That just might do the trick.

101

Here are a few things about paint pens that are useful to know:

✳ They are typically more permanent than other markers are. They have paint inside of them that adheres to the top of the surface, creating a smooth line.

✳ They come in different colors, including white and metallic colors (like gold!). When the surface you are drawing on is dark, white or metallic paint pens are great to use to make sure the lettering shows up.

✳ They also come in different tip sizes, from extra fine all the way to bold. To help you decide which size to buy, think about where you plan to use the pen and how big you want the lines of your letters to be. The examples below show the line sizes of the extra fine, fine, and medium points of the Sharpie Oil-Based Paint Pens.

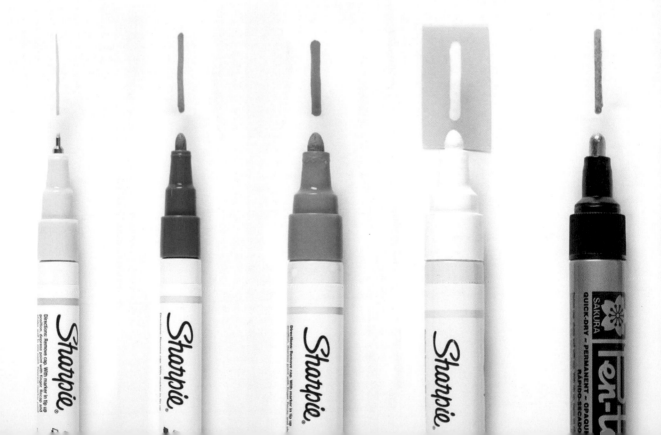

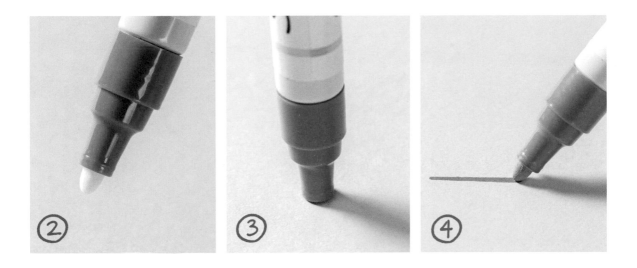

You'll notice that paint pens can't be used right when you first open the cap. Here's how to get them started:

1) With the cap on, shake the pen up and down for about 30 seconds. There is a tiny ball inside that mixes the paint when you shake it.

2) Take off the cap. The tip will be an off-white color like in the first image, without any paint yet.

3) On scratch paper, push the tip of the pen down so it disappears back into the pen. Hold it there for a few seconds and then let it go. When you release, you will start to see the paint filling into the tip.

If you don't see anything happening, put the cap back on and try shaking the pen again, then press down on the tip one or two more times. Don't push too many times or else the pen may drip with paint.

4) Once the paint color is fully covering the tip, test out the pen and draw a line. You do not need to press down hard, and you can draw the same way you do with a regular pen. The paint should be a solid color, and from there you can letter away!

Now that you know how to start your paint pen, let's put it to use! For this project, dream big and think outside the box. Have you ever tried to write on a leaf or a rock? Is there anything in your backyard or a local park that you can pick up and use as a canvas? Whatever you choose, make sure you have something besides paper to write on for this project.

SUPPLIES:

O   leaves

O   rocks

O   scratch paper

O   pencil

O   tape

O   paint pen

1) First, brainstorm some ideas of what to write on your found object:

   • *If you're drawing on leaves, you can write your friend's name to give them as a token of kindness.*

   • *If you're drawing on a rock, an idea is to write* You Rock! *and use it to hold your papers down at your school desk. Or you could write a welcome note on a big rock and place it at the front door of your home.*

2) Take out scratch paper and practice your word(s) first. You have many hand-lettering styles you can write with now, so take time to experiment.

3) Clean your found object of any dirt or other debris.

4) If you're writing on a leaf, use removable tape to tape the leaf down to the table as you write.

5) Grab your paint pen and test it out on scratch paper first to make sure it is working. If your leaves or rocks are small, I would choose a thinner paint pen to use.

6) As you are drawing on your found object, if you notice the ink color is light, pause for a moment and take a look at the rocks in this photo. You'll notice the first rock is lighter in color and that each rock below it gets brighter and brighter in color. When you draw on different surfaces like rocks, the paint may need a few coats in order to show up as bright as it can. So, go back to your found object and add a few more coats if needed by tracing over the letters again and again.

If the paint isn't staying, try a different paint pen. Each brand of paint pen works differently, and sometimes you have to try other ones before you find the one that works best on your found object.

7) Finally, find a home for your found objects and enjoy what you just made!

The next time you want to use your paint pen for a new project, if it doesn't work, try shaking the pen. You need to wake up the paint for it to flow again. Remember to test it out on scratch paper, just in case the pen starts to drip when you use it again!

HIGH FIVE!

Do me a favor and take a break for a second. Go find the first word you wrote when you started this book and compare it to the last word or project you made in Lesson 11. Can you see the difference? I bet you can! Look at how much you have learned from the last 11 lessons and projects. And to think you are only halfway through the book!

Every time you practice hand lettering, your own style evolves. It might not be obvious to you at first, but when you compare what you did just now to your lettering when you first started, you'll see the difference. Give yourself a pat on the back. I'm also sending you a big high five for all your hard work!

xo, Nicole

LESSON
#12

CURSIVE
SCRIPT

That hand-lettering style toolbox of yours is getting pretty big now, and we're not done adding to it. For this lesson, you're going to learn yet another style—cursive. You might think of cursive as the formal handwriting your parents use. Yes, that is true, but it's also a fun style you can use to decorate your world. Cursive script is different than print hand lettering because the letters are connected together. It looks like one long word without any space between the letters, like you see in the *time to shine* art below.

Take a look at the ABCs on page 110. Then, flip back to page 19 and look at the first ABCs we practiced in this book. They look very similar, but what is different about them?

CURSIVE HAND LETTERING

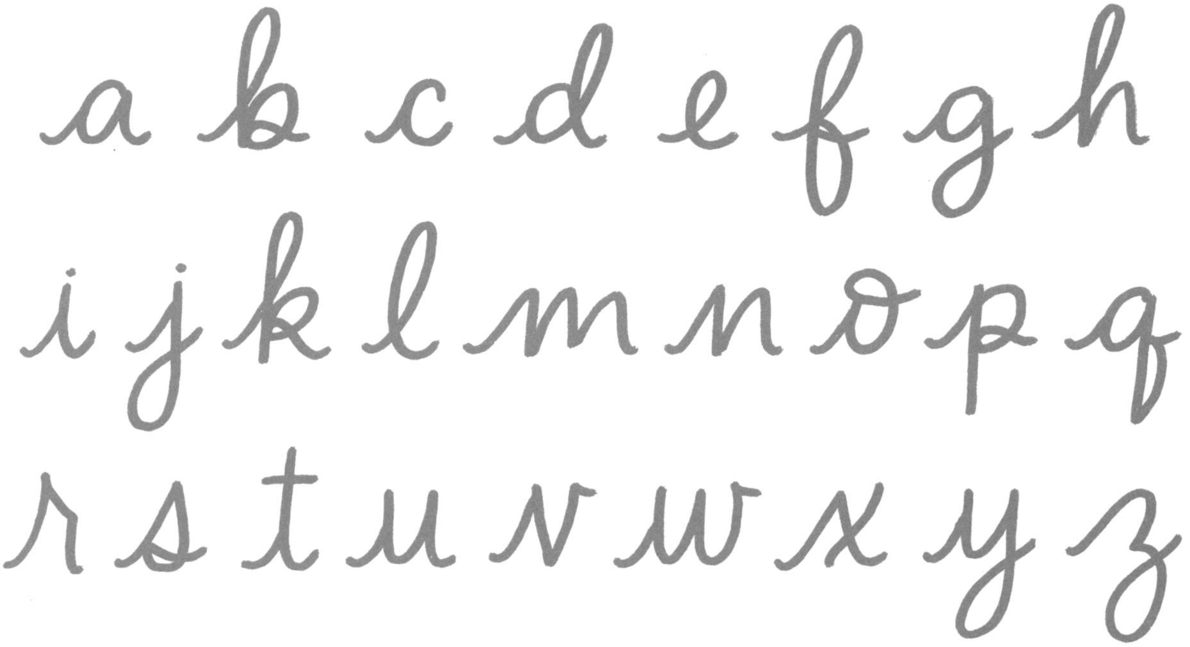

a b c d e f g h

i j k l m n o p q

r s t u v w x y z

If you answered that they have an extra tail or curve at the beginning of the letters, then you are exactly right! This is what will help to connect your letters and write in cursive. There are also four letters that look very different: the *f*, *r*, *s*, and *z*. Keep this page bookmarked as you practice so you can come back and look at the cursive letters. You don't have to memorize them at the moment.

f = f   r = r   s = s   z = z

Take out some scratch paper and practice these cursive letters on your own. If you already learned cursive in school, you can practice the way you know how to draw those letters.

Once you've done that a few times, let's put these cursive letters together and break down one way to learn this script style.

Step 1:

First, write out each letter of the word in the cursive style you just practiced, with small spaces in between.

friends

Can you see how the tails of the letters are almost touching one another? For example, the end tail of the *f* is almost touching the beginning tail of the *r*. Likewise, the end tail of the *r* is almost touching the beginning tail of the *i*.

Step 2:

Cursive script looks like one long word because the letters blend into one another. Use another pen and draw over the tails of your letters so they overlap, touching one another. This will fill the spaces. It's okay if your tails don't line up perfectly. Draw curved lines like you see below to create smooth connections between the letters.

friends

Before you go any further, did you happen to do Step 1 with your printed ABCs instead of your cursive ABCs? It's okay if you did! I just want to show you if you are having trouble with Step 2.

When trying to connect the letters together in *friends* below, there aren't any tails to link. The connection is harsh, especially with the *r* and *s*. So, instead of using the print ABCs, start with the cursive ABCs, and it will help make a smooth connection.

friends friends

Step 3:

Now that you know how each letter connects to the next, draw the entire word again all at once. You have two options:

* If you are using scratch paper, place your paper on top of the word you made in Step 2 with the added connecting lines. Trace what you see underneath, drawing the connected word all together.

* If you do not want to trace, have your word from Step 2 in front of you and copy what you see. This will help you know how to connect the letters to make your word look like it flows together.

friends

Finally, take a step back and look at what you have created. You started with individual letters and ended with one long cursive word. You did it!

Let's practice with one more word before starting your next project. Follow these steps to write *family* in cursive script:

Step 1:
Write out the letters.

family

Step 2:
Connect the tails.

family

Step 3:
Write the word one more time with the letters all connected.

family

Great job! You can see how these steps help to create a seamless flow from one letter to the next. Step 3 looks like you wrote the word all in one fluid motion.

TIP

This is a basic introduction to cursive script and only one way of learning how to write this way. If you are looking to learn more, there are a few books listed in the "Resources" section in the back of the book.

PROJECT #12
PICTURE FRAME

best friends

Great job learning cursive! It's now time to apply your new skills to a project. Have you seen any picture frames that have words on them? Maybe one of the family photos in your home says family or love? *Well, now you can make your own picture frame with your own hand lettering!*

SUPPLIES:

O   pictures

O   frame

O   scratch paper

O   pencil

O   pen/marker

O   scissors

O   tape

O   paint pen

O   paper towel

1)   Do you like taking pictures with your friends? Have you printed any of those photos out recently? If you haven't, that's okay—now is the time to print some out. It's fun to hold your memories in your hand!

2)   Next, find a picture frame to put your photo in. There are many different sizes and colors for you to choose from. Open up the frame and put your photo inside.

3)   Decide what to write on your frame. Maybe the words *best friends* or *family*? Practice your words on scratch paper in cursive, and go through Steps 1 to 3 on page 111.

If you don't like cursive script, you can always write with any of the other hand-lettering styles you learned in this book.

4)   Once you have your final words on practice paper, use scissors and cut out each word, like in the photos on page 116. Leave a little bit of white space around each one. These are going to help you imagine where you want to write your words.

5)   Put your frame from Step 2 flat on the table and place your cut-out words on top of the frame. Move them around to see what they will

look like in different places. For example, move the cut-out words to the top-left corner, like in the photo to the left. Or try them in the bottom-right corner. For this project, we will write on the clear outside part of the frame so your words can overlap the photo without messing it up.

If your cut-out words are too big and don't fit on the frame, rewrite the words on practice paper, but smaller this time. Cut the words out and go through the same steps to decide where you want to draw your design.

6) Pick up the cut-out words and place them on the table. Then, flip the frame over and open it up to take out the clear part. Be careful if it is glass. Lay the clear part on the table.

7) Now, take your cut-out words and tape them underneath the glass where you want to write. Have the lettering face up like in the photo to the right, so you can see through the clear part to trace. Now you have a stencil.

8) Since the clear part of the frame is either glass or plastic, I suggest using a paint pen. Flip back to Lesson 11 if you need a reminder of what paint pens are. Shake your pen first and test it out before jumping right in. If you do not have paint pens, a Sharpie will work.

9) Place a paper towel on the corner or edge of the glass. Then, use your paint pen and trace over your cursive lettering. You are writing on the clear glass part because the paper stencil is on the other side.

10) Once that is complete, remove the tape and words from underneath and place the glass or plastic back in the frame. Close the frame up and flip it over.

11) You now have your very own picture frame! If you love it so much that you want to keep it yourself, go through these steps again and make one for your friend. You can have matching frames and some fun memories to always keep close to you.

LESSON
#13

CONNECTING
IN CURSIVE

In the last lesson you learned how to write in cursive script. Now, let's dive in a little deeper and continue learning about this hand-lettering style. Take out some scratch paper and write out the phrase *hip hip hooray* in cursive on your own.

I also wrote out this phrase and followed the steps from Lesson 12, drawing each individual letter first in the cursive style. But when I got to Step 2 (connecting the tails), I noticed that the tail after the o's in *hooray* were hard to connect. Take a look below. The end of the first *o* is high, and the beginning of the second *o* is low.

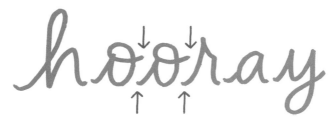

When I try to add the overlapping line connecting the tails, it isn't really smooth, as shown in the example below. Did this happen to you, too?

Let's problem solve. Our first option is to go low and bring the ending tail of the first *o* down to reach the beginning tail of the second *o*.

Or, we can go high and keep the ending tail up on the *o* as it is. In this option, we can then change the beginning tail of the second *o* to be drawn up to meet the connecting line.

The same movement of going high also works for the *o-r* connection.

When comparing the two options, since the *o* in the first *hooray* (when we went low) gets cut off and the line goes through the middle of the letter, I prefer the second option (going high). This is because it has a cleaner look. I wrote *hooray* once more below to see it all together. Looks great!

Now, let's see if going high with the tails also works with the word *love*:

Step 1: Write out the letters.

Step 2: Connect the tails.

It looks like we have the same situation where the ends don't line up for the *o-v* tails and the *v-e* tails.

But if we go high like we tried in *hooray* and move the beginnings of the *v* and *e* up, it looks like it can work.

Step 3: Write the word one more time. Going high works again!

To recap, as you connect your cursive letters, if you find yourself getting stuck at any point, try this—go high. Think of cursive script as a friendship, and all of the letters are friends. What do you do when your friend is having a hard day? You reach out a hand, give her a hug, and try to lift her spirits up (not bring her down). You can support her by going high, and the same goes for your letters!

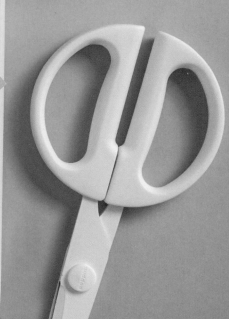

PROJECT #13
GIFT TAGS

to:
Julie
from:
Nicole

When you give a gift to someone, do you like to wrap it in a box, or put it in a bag? After this project, you will be able to add a handmade gift tag to give it that final personal touch!

SUPPLIES:

- O cardstock or watercolor paper

- O scissors

- O hole punch

- O scratch paper

- O pencil

- O watercolors + wide brush (optional)

- O marker/gel pen/brush pen/paint pen

- O string

1) Grab some cardstock, scissors, and a hole punch, or if you have pre-made blank tags from the store like the ones shown on the candy favors on page 126 you can use those too.

2) Decide what to write on your gift tags. Some ideas are phrases like *hugs to you* and *open me*, or you can write *to* and *from* and leave space to add in the names later on.

3) To make your own tags, place scratch paper over the templates on page 125. You can do all three or pick your favorite one. Then, cut them out to use as your stencils.

4) Choose your cardstock to make the final tags. Think of the person for whom you are making the gift tags. Do you know her or his favorite color? Or do you want to make watercolor-wash tags? If so, use watercolor paper and revisit Lesson 5.

5) Once you have your cardstock, place your stencil on top and outline the shape in pencil. Then, cut the tags out.

6) Dig into your toolbox and pick a pen. You can use markers, brush pens, gel pens, or even paint pens if you want to write in white like the *open me* tag on page 123. Draw your phrase on each gift tag, and don't worry about messing up; you can always cut out more tags!

7) If you want to add more, draw symbols around the words to fill in the space. You can also make more tags with just patterns on them to add a fun extra pop.

8) Finally, punch a hole in the top and add string to tie the tags to your presents. Those little tags will make the recipient feel warm and fuzzy even before they open up the gift inside!

TEMPLATES

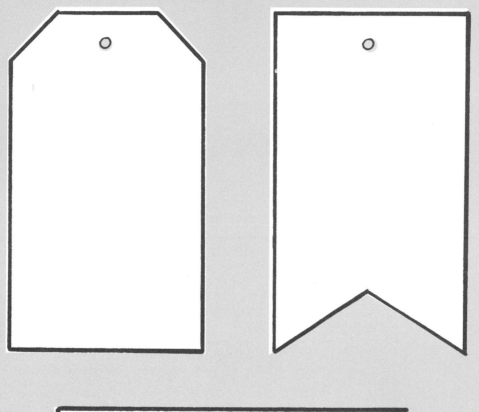

TRY, TRY + TRY AGAIN

Look at you go! I know this is a lot of information, and you're learning a lot of new things. As you continue practicing your hand lettering and doing these projects, there may be some moments when you feel stuck.

What pen do I use? What paper works best? How do I make my letters look like that?

Here's something for you to remember: trial and error. This means that you can try again if your letters don't look how you want them to and do something different. Ask yourself, *is there a different pen I can use? Or is there another type of material I need? Or can I try connecting my letters in a different way so the word reads smoothly?*

If you have to start over, it doesn't mean you failed or that you did something wrong. It means that you tried and came across an error. But you can always try again. Errors are how you grow— they are good things as far as I am concerned.

Keep on making. Keep on experimenting. Try, try, and try again. I'm cheering you on!

xo, Nicole

LESSON #14

FLOURISHES

When you get dressed in the morning, how do you pick your outfit? Do you start by choosing the top—T-shirt or tank top, short sleeve or long sleeve? Does that decision then help you decide what bottoms to wear—jeans, leggings, shorts, or a skirt? There are also many options of accessories to choose from. Do you wear a necklace, a bracelet, or earrings? Do you add anything in your hair or wear a baseball hat? These options are all extras that can be added and are part of your personality!

So, how does this relate to hand lettering? Think of your hand-lettering style as your outfit. You can decide to draw your letters angled or straight, circular or oval, just like when you choose what top and bottom to wear before you go to school. Both your letters and your outfit are the essentials.

Then, you have the extras—the accessories—that you add on. And for your hand lettering, the accessories are extra curves, loops, and swirls called flourishes.

Can you see the difference between the two *outfit* examples below? The first one has a straight line crossing the *t*, while the second one has an extra curve on the line crossing the *t*. This extra curve is the accessory added on—the flourish. Both are great options—you have the choice to add on the extra curve or leave the crossing of the *t* straight.

Let's practice some on your own. Flourishes can be swoops and loops, curls and twists. They can be as long or as short as you'd like. Take out scratch paper and draw these flourishes.

Once you have practiced, let's learn a little bit about *when* to use them. Take a look at *happy birthday* below—this is the outfit and the starting point.

happy birthday

We already learned that a flourish can come in the form of crossing the *t* with a curve, so let's add that to our word.

happy birthday

Another spot where you can add a flourish is at the end of a word. Extend the *y*'s like you see below to loop back up.

happy birthday

Don't forget to give some love to the beginning of the word, too. Let's try adding a loop to the beginnings of the *h* and the *b*. That's fun!

happy birthday

Now, you have several additional loops and curves that add to your hand-lettered word. Think of flourishes as extensions of your letters. They add to the foundation of your outfit and bring out the beauty of your letters. They are true accessories! Continue practicing with some words of your own. Ask yourself if you can add any flourishes to the beginning, middle, or end of the words.

PROJECT #14
RIBBON

Now that you're thinking about accessories, how about making some ribbon with your hand lettering on it? You can use ribbon as a bow in your hair, to tie around your wrist as a friendship bracelet, or to add onto your backpack. Ribbon is also great to wrap your presents and use with the gift tags you made in Project 13.

SUPPLIES:

O **ribbon**

O **scissors**

O **hair spray**

O **paper towels**

O **scratch paper**

O **pencil**

O **gel pen**

O **removable tape**

1) First, you'll need the ribbon. Maybe someone in your family has extra ribbon lying around the house that is used for wrapping presents. Or if you go to a store, pick out some fun colors and varying widths. I suggest buying a few types of ribbon because there are different kinds with unique textures. This means your pens may react differently to the different textures when you try to write on them.

2) Figure out the length of ribbon you will need. If you're making friendship bracelets, wrap the ribbon around your own wrist and add a little extra so you can tie a knot at the end. Then, cut it to that length.

3) Ribbon is made up of tiny pieces that are threaded together. This creates tiny holes that your eye may not even see. Because of this, when you draw on your ribbon, you might notice the ink spreading out more than it does when you write on paper. To prevent this from happening, I have a trick for you: hair spray.

Lay out paper towels to make a space that can get dirty and place your ribbon on top of that. Ask an adult to help you use the hair spray. Hold the hair-spray can several inches away from the ribbon and then lightly spray a coat on it. Let the ribbon dry completely.

4) While the ribbon is drying, practice your lettering. Since this lesson was on flourishes, try to add some to your own words. Remember that flourishes are loops and swirls that can be added to the beginning or end of your words and also when you cross a *t*. If it helps, trace the outline and size of the ribbon on scratch paper to make yourself a template and then draw your words within that area.

without hair spray

with hair spray

5) When your ribbon is dry, test out your pens on the ends of the ribbon. I suggest using gel pens instead of markers or brush pens. Paint pens are another option; however, sometimes the ink spreads out on the ribbon (even if you used hair spray). Gel pens come in all different colors and draw a bright line on the ribbon.

6) Use removable tape to secure the ends of the ribbon to the table. Then, slowly and lightly draw your words on the ribbon. You do not need to press very hard to write with gel pens. Repeat and make more for your friends to share.

7) Finally, tie the ribbon around your hair to make a bow. Or, if you made friendship bracelets, wrap the ribbons around the wrists of you and your friends and tie knots to finish them off. You now have cool new accessories to share with everyone!

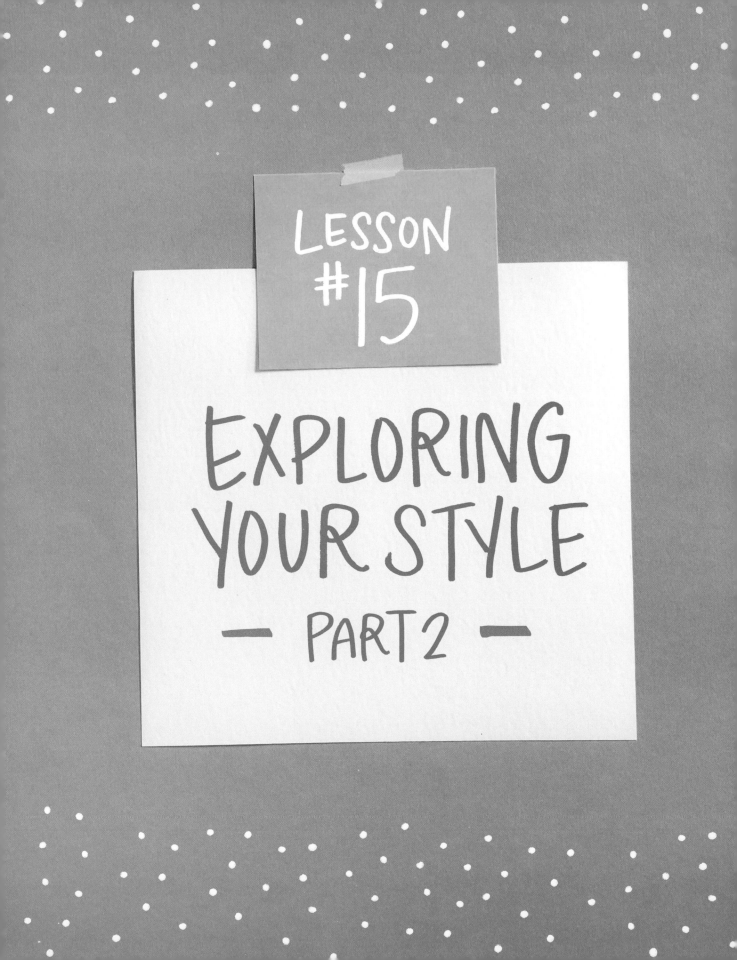

LESSON #15

EXPLORING YOUR STYLE
— PART 2 —

You started this book by focusing on your print style of lettering. Then, you learned several ways to change your hand lettering to make new styles. And in Lesson 10, you combined some of those earlier lessons of playing with the space between the letters (Lesson 9), changing the angle (Lesson 8), and drawing with different shapes (Lesson 4).

Now you're going to do the same thing, but with your cursive script.

To refresh your memory, you can use the scale below to help you create different hand-lettering styles. The icons on the scale represent what you can experiment with. The spacing can go from tight (ABC) to wide (A B C); the angle can go from straight (|||) to slanted (///); and the shape can go from circular (OOO) to oval (OOO).

Look at the three different ways to write *beautiful* in cursive on the next page and observe where the heart is on each line. The first *beautiful* has medium spacing, straight angles, and circular-shaped letters. The second *beautiful* has tight spacing, straight angles, and oval-shaped letters. The third *beautiful* has wide spacing, slanted angles, and oval-shaped letters. Each of these options is a new style of cursive script you can experiment with.

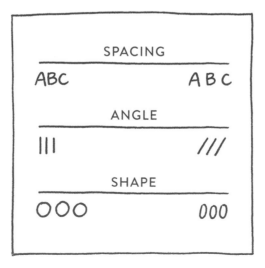

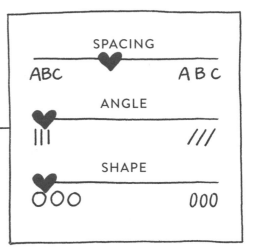

beautiful

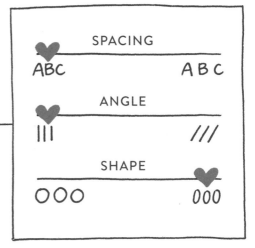

beautiful

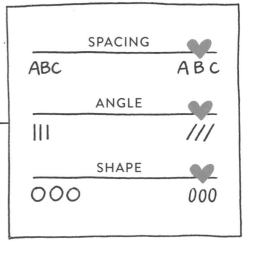

beautiful

Try this out with your name. First, write it how you normally write in cursive. Then, looking at what you wrote, where would your hearts be placed on the scales of *spacing*, *angle*, and *shape*? Make your own scale and draw your hearts. From there, you can start adjusting your style.

Here's an example with the name *Chloe* as written below.

Chloe

Looking at this version of *Chloe*, the spacing is medium, the angle is straight, and the shape of the letters is circular. Now, I'll try writing *Chloe* again, but this time I will pretend to move the heart of the spacing scale all the way to the right to have wide spacing. The result is the *Chloe* below.

Chloe

Then, if I pretend to move the heart all the way to the other side, to the left on the spacing scale, the next version of *Chloe* will have tight spacing. This result is the *Chloe* below.

Chloe

Looking at all three examples, you can see how they reflect three different styles. Your next step can be to change just the angle and go from there.

TIP

To help you draw your letters at an angle, you can use the angled grid on page 81 by placing it under your paper to help guide you. Lesson 8 is also there to refresh your memory!

PROJECT #15

TENT NAME CARDS

Ready for a simple and quick project that can bring the biggest smiles to your friends' and family's faces? Tent place cards are a fun option for adding names to the dinner table. All you have to do is fold a paper in half and add your beautiful hand lettering!

SUPPLIES:

- ○ scratch paper

- ○ pencil

- ○ cardstock or watercolor paper

- ○ scissors

- ○ watercolor + wide brush (optional)

- ○ marker/gel pen/brush pen/paint pen

1) Since names start with a capital letter, let's first practice how to draw capital letters in cursive. Take out scratch paper and turn to page 142. You'll see two styles: one with straight angles and one with slanted angles. Some of the letters are also different between the two sets to show you that there are other ways to write each letter. Maybe ask your parents or teacher how they would write their names in cursive. Everyone has a unique style.

2) Pick your paper to make the final place cards. You can pick colored cardstock, or if you want to add a fun watercolor wash to your place cards, use watercolor paper.

3) Tent cards can be any size. They can be tall or short, wide or skinny. If you like the ones in the photo, cut a rectangle that is 4 x 3.5 inches. Then, fold it in half to make a folded tent card that is 2 x 3.5 inches.

CURSIVE SCRIPT CAPITAL LETTERS

A B C D E F G H I
J K L M N O P Q R
S T U V W X Y Z

• • • • • • • • • •

A B C D E F G H I
J K L M N O P Q R
S T U V W X Y Z

4) If you are adding a watercolor wash (see Project 5 for a refresher), do that first and let the paper completely dry before lettering.

5) Since you are writing on paper, any markers or pens will do. But if you are using dark paper, remember that gel pens or paint pens are best since they will show up nice and bright. I used a white paint pen to write *Reese*'s name here. Write the name on the bottom section of the cardstock so, when you fold the cards, the name will not be upside down.

6) Add in the thick down stroke like you learned in Lesson 3 to make the names pop. If you make a mistake, you can easily make more tent cards!

7) When you're done, put the place cards on the plate or next to each place setting. Watch everyone's face light up with a smile when they see what you made!

LESSON #16

MIXING STYLES

Your hand-lettering toolbox is getting full! You are like a magician with magic tricks you can pull out of thin air at any moment.

For this lesson, we're going to use some of these tricks. To start, write out all the different ways you can think of drawing the word *the* on practice paper.

PRINT HAND LETTERING

CURSIVE SCRIPT

* Play with the shape (Lesson 4)

* Change the height of your letters (Lesson 5)

* Change the angle (Lesson 8)

* Add more space between the letters (Lesson 9)

* Add flourishes (Lesson 14)

That's a total of twelve different ways of hand lettering right there!

Now, try out different options for writing the word *family*.

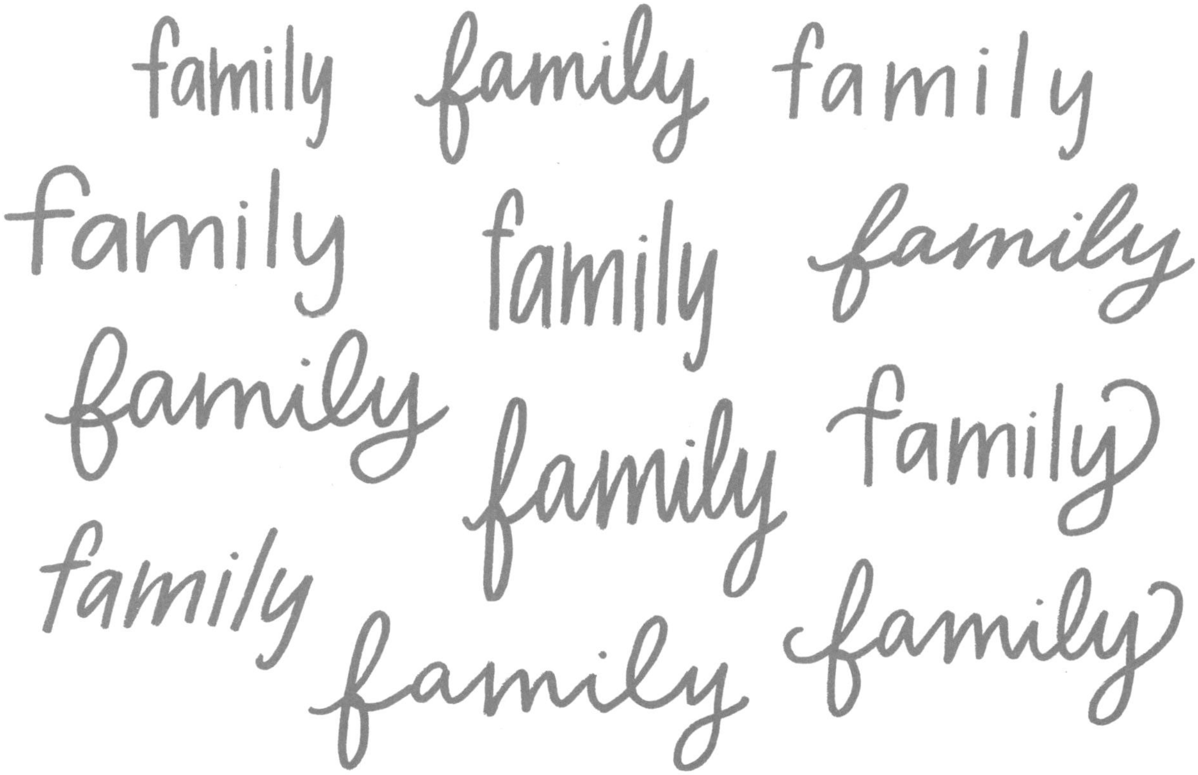

family *family* *family*

family *family* *family*

family *family* *family*

family *family* *family*

Finally, go through this exercise and write your last name in a few different styles. This time, write your last name a little bigger than the size you wrote *the* and *family*. Also, experiment with doing all print capital letters like you learned on page 21 and see if you like the look of that.

Once you are done, take a step back and look at what you made! You have become a designer who has created many hand-lettering styles!

For the next step, use scissors and cut out all of the words individually, leaving a little bit of white space around each one. This will help you prepare for your next project. You might have noticed you are making a sign that says *The (your last name) family.*

With all of your words spread out on a table, pick one of each word to create your layout. Think of it like a puzzle—a really great puzzle because you are the designer. Maybe all three words are in your cursive script, or perhaps all three are in your block style, or you can mix and match styles like the example below. Explore and see what combination makes you smile and feels right. Trust yourself and what your heart is telling you. Then, you can move on to the next project.

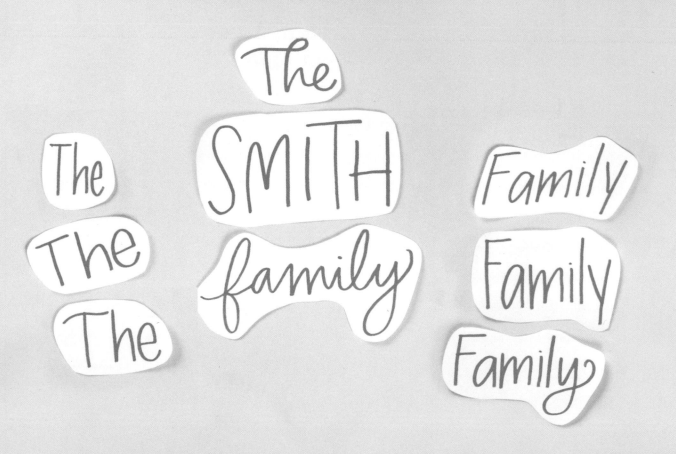

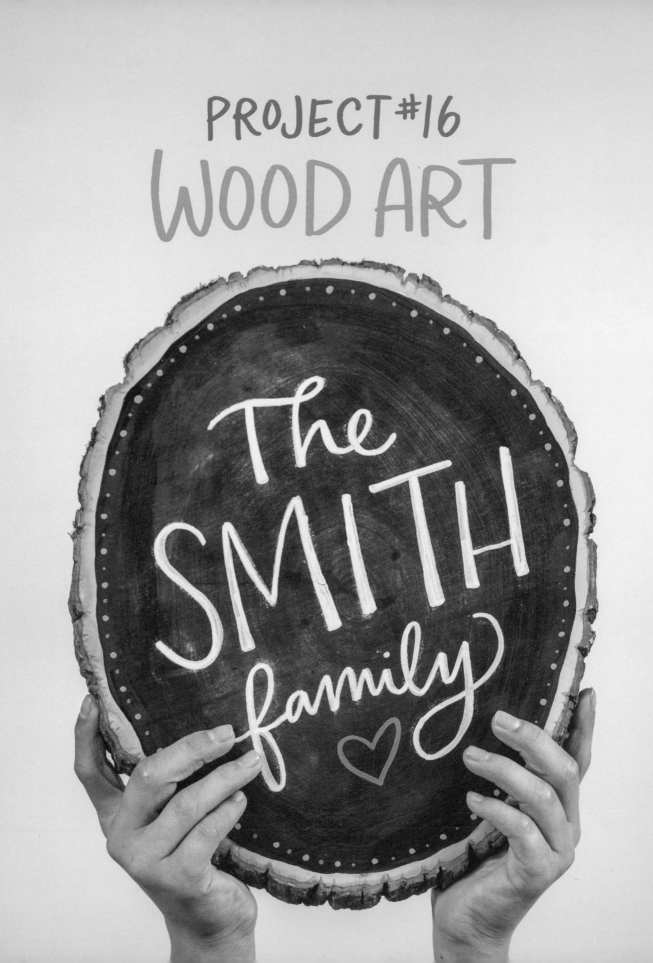

PROJECT #16
WOOD ART

The
SMITH
family

Although you most likely won't be able to walk outside and find a nice slab of wood to write on, there are stores and websites where you can purchase wood slices like you see in the photos here. Check the "Resources" section in the back for a list of places that sell wood slabs.

SUPPLIES:

O wood slice

O chalk paint or acrylic paint

O big paint brush for paint

O scratch paper

O chalk

O paper towel

O paint pen

O chalk pens (optional)

O clear matte spray (optional)

1) Decide what to draw on your wood sign. You already wrote your family name in the previous lesson, or, if you have a favorite quote you can practice on scratch paper first. Remember: You have a whole toolbox of styles you can choose from!

2) Most likely your wood is uncoated and raw like in the first photo on page 150. You can leave it raw or paint the background a color. If you decide to paint, use chalk paint or acrylic paint. Both can be purchased at craft or home improvement stores and come in different colors. Shake the can or bottle the paint comes in and use a big brush to paint on the flat surface. Once you have an even coat of paint, let it completely dry.

3) Have your cut-out words next to you from this lesson or the practice paper from Step 1 and find some chalk. Draw your design in chalk on the wood first so that if you want to change something, you can use a paper towel to rub that part off.

If your last name is longer, think about drawing the design horizontally instead of vertically.

4) To make your design permanent, use a paint pen and trace over your chalk lettering. Shake your pen to get it started and test it out on scratch paper. Review Lesson 11 if you need a refresher on paint pens. As you trace your lettering, it's okay if you smear

the chalk. It is just there as your stencil and will be fully removed in the next step.

5) Once your lettering is completely dry, use a dry paper towel to rub off any leftover chalk you can see. *Do not* use a damp paper towel as the paint may smudge if you use water.

6) Add any other patterns to your design, like a border or a heart. Paint pens come in different colors so have fun and add some personality to your sign.

7) If you want to really make your sign permanent, seal the wood with a clear matte spray. Ask an adult to help you do this, and be sure to spray outside.

8) Finally, find a home for your new sign and enjoy!

Another option for the lettering is to use chalk pens or to keep your lettering in chalk. This way you can erase and change your design whenever you want.

LESSON #17

DOODLES

Doodles. They are the quick scribbles you draw in class, or the little drawings you add on notes to your friends. But did you know that doodles can also be a useful tool for your hand lettering? They help you figure out your design and tap into your inner artist.

You'll be making cards for the project that goes with this lesson, so start thinking of a phrase or a quote that you want to add to a card. I'll be writing *You Are Awesome*, and you can absolutely use that phrase as well.

First, close your eyes and imagine the look of your final card. Do any ideas come to mind? Maybe your card is vertical, and each word is on its own line? Or perhaps your card is horizontal, and the design is written on two lines?

To help you see your options, draw your ideas as little quick doodles. First, draw a small rectangle to represent your card. Then, write your words inside the rectangle. Remember that doodles are rough and do not need to look pretty. This is your time to explore and get the ideas out of your head and onto paper. No idea is wrong.

Here are some additional ideas to get your thoughts flowing. You can draw your quote:

- On a diagonal

- In the shape of a circle

- On a curve or wave

You can also play with the lettering style. Think back to all that you learned in this book. You can:

- Use print lettering (Lesson 2)

- Make the letters more circular than oval (Lesson 4) or vice versa

- Change the angle (Lesson 8)

- Draw in cursive (Lesson 12)

- Use both print and cursive scripts (Lesson 16)

There are also patterns and symbols you can add to your design:

- Hearts

- Arrows

- Polka dots

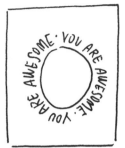

You have so many doodles and ideas you are trying out. Do you have a favorite one? These small drawings give you a sneak peek at what your final cards will look like. Once you are done, pick your favorite, or a few of them, to use on the next project.

PROJECT #17
CARDS

Handmade cards are a special way to send someone a message. They can be used for birthday thank-you notes, or just because you want to remind a friend that he or she is awesome!

Who is the person who bought you this book? You can make her or him a card to show all that you have learned and to say thank you.

SUPPLIES:

O cardstock or watercolor paper

O scissors

O watercolor + wide brush (optional)

O scratch paper

O pencil

O marker/gel pen/brush pen/paint pen

1) First, you can either buy pre-folded blank cards from a craft store or make your own. To make your own, measure a rectangle for example around 9 x 5.5 inches on cardstock or watercolor paper. Then, cut it out and fold in half.

2) If you want to add a watercolor wash (Lesson 5) to your card, do that now and give the paper time to completely dry.

3) Take out your doodles from this lesson. If you haven't done so already, draw a rectangle around your doodle. This will help you see what your final card will look like.

4) Then add any guidelines that might help you draw your design. For example, my doodle is written at a diagonal. So, in this step, I used a ruler (like in the photo on page 158) and drew two lines at a diagonal to help me know where to draw my words.

5) Use your lettering tools to draw your design on the final card.

- *You can use a pencil and lightly copy your design directly on the card first. Then, trace over it with your marker.*

- *You can freehand it using a marker only and skip the pencil step. If you do this, have your stencil from Step 5 next to you to refer to.*

- *You can use the trick you learned in Project 8 and find a window that has some light shining through it. Use a black marker and trace over your stencil from Step 5 to make it darker. Then, tape your stencil to the window and your cardstock over that to see the lettering through the paper. Now you can trace your design onto the final card.*

6) Once your design is complete, open it up and write a message on the inside. The next lesson is about making envelopes, so keep on reading and then you can mail your card to that special someone!

TiP

If you plan to draw at a diagonal or on a curve, it helps to draw guide-lines instead of trying to eyeball it.

PEP TALK

YOU HAVE YOUR OWN MARK

You may know this already, but I want to remind you that you are unique. No one in the world is just like you. And you know what that means? That means your hand lettering is going to be unique, too.

If you're reading this and wanting everything to be perfect and for your letters to look exactly like what you see in this book, repeat this to yourself: "I am unique, and I have my own mark in this world." Perfect isn't what we're going for here. You are designing your own hand lettering and making something beautiful out of nothing. And that makes you creative. Keep on expressing yourself and bringing your own flair and personality to your letters. And don't forget to have fun while doing this!

xo, Nicole

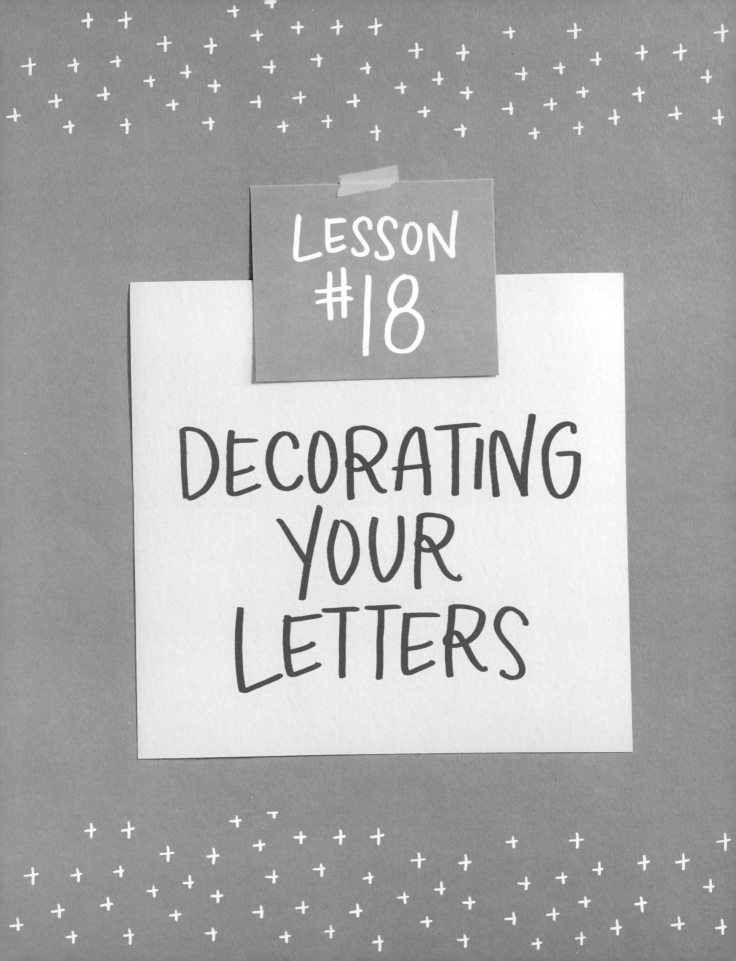

LESSON #18

DECORATING YOUR LETTERS

This lesson is all about you and the freedom to express yourself. Pull out all the pens and markers from your toolbox, and let's learn new ways to decorate your hand lettering!

LINES INSIDE:

Use one of your thicker pens to draw your word first. Then, using a smaller pen in a different color, draw a thin line in the center. If your letters are dark, the white gel pen is a great option to use here and will make your letters shine brightly!

If you used the thin and thick lettering style you learned in Lesson 3, another idea is to add the line to just the thick down parts of the letters. This will create some bounce and movement across the whole word like in *Emily* below.

DOTS INSIDE:

Another way to decorate your letters is to add dots on the inside of the lines. This also works best if your lines are thicker. Use a different color to accent the letters or use a gold gel pen or a gold paint pen to add a little sparkle. Fun, right?

DOTS ON THE OUTSIDE:

This time, instead of drawing the dots inside your letters, draw them on the outside of your word. You can do this in any color, and it will add a fun pop to your letters. It might even look like it's a sign on a billboard!

BUBBLES:

If you aren't tired of dots yet, add a dot to the beginning and end of each letter. They can either be filled in or open. This makes a bubbly and fun type of lettering!

HEARTS:

Instead of dots, add hearts to the ends of your letters. You can choose to add a heart to every spot where you see an end or just draw one heart on each letter.

Isabella

McKenzie

SHADOWS:

First, use a darker pen or marker to write your word. Let that dry for a few moments. While you're waiting, look at the examples below. Can you see how the pink and yellow lines are drawn to the right of the original word? Using a lighter-color pen, write your word again, but this time write it slightly to the right. This way, part of the line will show up like you see here.

Caden Emma

You now have so many new ways to decorate your hand lettering. What fun!

PROJECT #18
ENVELOPES

Chloe Jones
5221 STARFISH BLVD.
SAN DIEGO, CA 92130

your address
goes here

Forever
USA

add postage
stamps

Ever Winston
211 CORAL DR.
SAN DIEGO, CALIFORNIA 92130

the recipient's
address goes here

In the last project, you made a beautiful card, and now you are ready to deliver it. Instead of just handing it to him or her, why not make an envelope? This is like gift wrapping for cards, and you can decorate your envelope with the new styles you just practiced!

SUPPLIES:

O   envelopes

O   marker/gel pen/brush pen/paint pen

O   scratch paper

O   postage stamps (optional)

O   highlighters

O   glue stick

1) There are many different sizes and colors of envelopes for you to choose from. You don't need a specific envelope as long as your card fits inside.

2) Think about the person you are sending the card to:

   a.   Do they live close to you?

   b.   Are you going to see her or him within the week?

If your answer to either question is yes, this project is going to be short for you. Write the person's name on the outside of the envelope. Then, add decorations to your letters, like those from this lesson. Place your card inside the envelope, seal it shut, and the next time you see that person, give her or him the card.

3) If your answer is no to either of those questions, find out his or her mailing address, as you will be sending the card through the mail.

When you mail an envelope, there are a few things that it will need:

* *Postage stamps so the mail can go through the postal system. These go in the upper-right corner and can be purchased at the post office or online. If your card seems larger than usual, I suggest going to the post office with an adult to have the card weighed. It might need a special stamp.*

- *The person's name and address who is receiving the letter. This is written front and center. You can mix up the lettering styles and fill in the open space around the words by adding polka dots or starburst lines. Just be mindful that there will be a person on the other side reading the envelope, so the address needs to be clearly visible.*

- *A return address just in case the mail gets lost and needs to make its way back to you. It will go either in the upper-left corner on the front of the envelope, or on the back flap. Your name and address should be smaller than the recipient's address.*

4) Did you know you can also decorate the inside of your envelope? Open up the top flap (it may be pointy or square).

- *Can you feel the sort of sticky part on the edge of the flap? That is the glue that helps to seal the envelope shut. So, be sure to avoid that part.*

- *Use your marker and draw a pattern on the inside of the flap. You can see a few fun ideas of patterns to draw below.*

5) There is one more decorating step you can add. Close your envelope and flip it over to the back. Take scratch paper and place it beneath only the flap, like in the photo below. Use a highlighter and draw a line along the edge of the flap. It is okay if you draw on the scratch paper, too. Then, remove the scratch paper and look at the cool flap you just made!

6) Put your card inside the envelope and seal it shut. I like to use a glue stick on top of the glue edge to make sure it's really nice and sealed.

7) Finally, place the envelope in the mailbox. It may take a few days to a couple of weeks to arrive, depending on the letter's final destination. How cool to think that something you made is out there being delivered and will bring a smile to the face of the person you mailed it to!

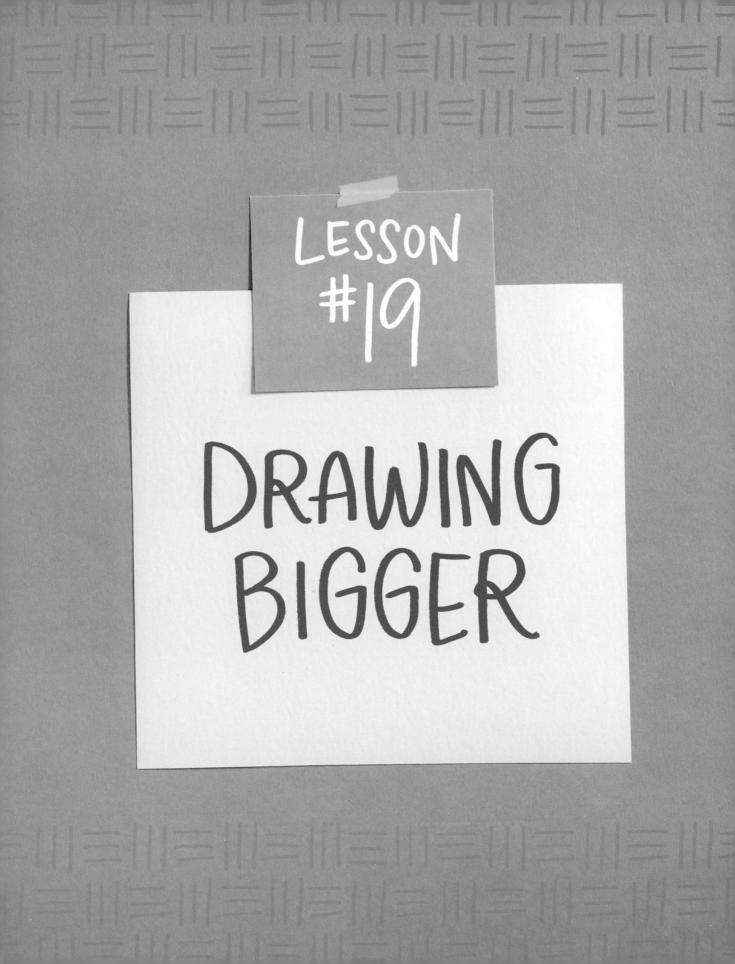

LESSON #19

DRAWING BIGGER

Have you ever looked at something handmade and thought, *how did they make that?* Maybe you're looking at the tote bag here and thinking, *that's so big—how did she get her lettering to be bigger?* I have the answer for you in this lesson. This one is going to be a little different than the others, combining the lesson *with* the project. Be sure to grab your supplies first so we can dive right into making this cool tote bag.

PROJECT #19
TOTE BAGS

SUPPLIES:

O scratch paper

O pencil/pen

O tote bag (a light-colored tote bag is best)

O light-colored marker

O dark-colored marker

O painter's or masking tape

O fabric pen or Sharpie

Step 1: *Doodles*

1) In Lesson 17, you learned how doodles help to get all of the ideas for your design out of your head and onto paper. Let's try that again. Have scratch paper and a pen or pencil to doodle with. Pick a quote or follow along with *Dream Big* that I'm using here.

2) Hold your tote bag up in front of you to help you imagine your design. Ask yourself the following questions:

- *Do you see your bag with all the words really big?*

- *Do you imagine one word bigger than the other?*

- *Can you experiment with having both print lettering and your cursive script?*

These are just a few questions you can ask yourself to get your ideas flowing. Draw your quick doodles on scratch paper to see all of your options. Remember your hand-lettering toolbox of styles you have learned. Make the letters more circular (Lesson 4), draw them at an angle (Lesson 8), or spread the spacing out (Lesson 9).

Step 2: *Make a Stencil*

1) After getting all of your ideas down on paper, pick your favorite doodle. If you didn't already, draw a vertical rectangle around that one. This is a mini version of what your tote bag will look like.

2) Take out another piece of scratch paper to use as your stencil. This entire sheet is going to help you draw your design bigger.

3) Have your final doodle next to you and use that as your guide. On your full piece of scratch paper, draw the letters bigger to fill up the entire space.

4) After trying this out on your own, it's okay if you found this difficult. It's not easy for me either! I have a trick for you. First, on your small doodle, draw a vertical line down the center and a horizontal line across the center of your design. This breaks your doodle into four sections, as you can see in the drawing below.

5) Then, take a new piece of scratch paper and fold it in half. Open it up and fold it in half the other way. Use a lighter-colored marker and draw a line over the folds to see the creases more easily. Can you see the four smaller rectangles you made by

folding the paper in half? Now, look back at your doodle with the grid lines over it. Can you see the same four smaller rectangles there, too?

6) Instead of drawing the full design like you first tried in step 3, you are now going to draw the design section by section. Think of this as four parts of the whole.

7) Start with the upper-left section of the stencil. Look at your doodle first and draw what you see in just that section, transferring it onto the bigger stencil you folded and made

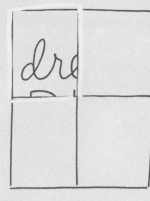
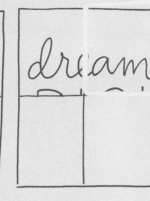
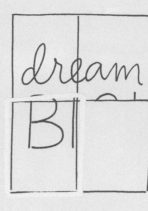

in Step 4. You are drawing the lines you see and not the full word, just like in the photo on page 172.

8) Then, copy just what you see in the upper-right section of your doodle onto the big stencil.

9) Continue with the bottom left section.

10) Finally, draw the bottom right section to complete your stencil. Hold it up, and hopefully you can see your entire quote! You just went from a small doodle to this bigger drawing. Great job!

If you need to line up a few parts and connect the letters, go ahead and do that now.

11) If you completed the last steps in pencil or a light-colored pen, draw over the entire quote in a darker thick pen. This will make sense in the next step.

Step 3: *Drawing on the Tote Bag*

1) You are now ready to make your final bag. Put the stencil you just made inside your bag so you can see the quote through the front material. This is so you can trace.

If you don't see your stencil through the front of the bag, the fabric may be too thick, or the fabric color may be too dark. That's okay. Simply use a pencil or chalk and draw your quote directly on the outside of the bag. This will be your stencil instead.

2) Tape your stencil inside the bag and then tape your bag to the table to keep it in place while you draw.

3) Since the tote bag is fabric, I suggest using a fabric pen to draw for this project. A Sharpie may also work, but remember, some pens will bleed on certain fabrics. Fabric pens can be found at craft stores and come in different colors. Trace your quote and watch your bag come to life!

4) If you want to add a little more flair, draw a heart somewhere, or an arrow, or draw multi-colored polka dots around your words. Have fun and enjoy your new tote bags to carry your favorite things!

CELEBRATE!

PROJECT #20
BALLOONS

Guess what? You made it to your last project in this book—big high five for that! Your only assignment for this lesson is to have fun. Blow up some balloons, invite your friends over, and celebrate! And yes, you can actually write on balloons!

SUPPLIES:

○ balloons

○ helium tank (optional)

○ string

○ scissors

○ paint pens

1) First, blow up your balloons. If you want them to float, you'll need a helium tank to blow them up with. Ask an adult to help you, or you can buy balloons at a store already blown up.

2) After you blow up each balloon, tie a knot at the bottom and add string.

3) Have somewhere you can tie the other end of the string, so the balloons don't float away. Sometimes I tie the strings to a nearby chair or something else that is heavy.

4) Now that your hands are free, grab your paint pens. I recommend the medium to large bold-tip paint pens because they draw a thicker line. Shake the paint pen to get it started and test it out on scratch paper. Flip back to page 101 if you need a refresher on paint pens.

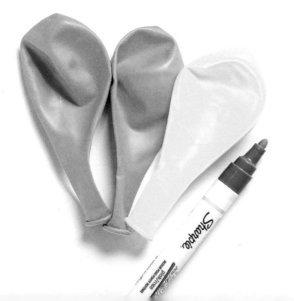

178

5) You are probably aware that balloons can pop. So, please know that this can happen at any moment. As you write on your balloons, keep these suggestions in mind to help you avoid popping your balloon:

- *Don't put too much pressure on the balloon when writing. What I found works best for support is to write on a table that is right next to a wall. This way, you can lean the balloon against the wall and have your non-writing hand hold it there. This will help keep the balloon stable as you write.*

- *Be careful that the tip doesn't catch on the balloon and pierce it. Try writing with more of the side of the pen than the pointed tip.*

6) Continue to add your hand lettering to the balloon. You have so many words you've practiced in this book and so many ways to add decorations. Draw whatever makes your heart smile. Maybe draw just a smiley face on one or add a pattern to another one. This is your time to celebrate and have fun!

Conclusion

You did it! You made it to the end of this book. Well done! But that doesn't mean your hand-lettering journey stops here.

All the projects in this book are designed so that you can go back and make more at any time. You now have so many hand-lettering styles that you can use, and the lessons are always there as a refresher.

The next time you need to make a gift for someone, open these pages and find a project to make. Or, if it's a rainy day and you feel bored, grab your toolbox of pens and markers and color using one of your hand-lettering styles. And if you ever find that you need to express yourself and get the beautiful ideas out of your head, remember you can draw little doodles and turn them into your own masterpieces!

My challenge to you is to open your eyes and take in inspiration from what's around you. Look at the beautiful colors in Mother Nature, write down that quote you heard someone say that made you smile, and be aware of the people around you. If you notice someone is having a hard day, maybe you can hand letter that person's name on a note. Make an envelope and remind that person of how awesome they are. Then, you can invite your friend to make some projects with you after school and learn hand lettering.

Everyone has his or her own unique hand-lettering style, and it's fun to decorate your life with your friends by your side. Keep making this world a little brighter, one letter at a time!

HAND-LETTERING STYLE TOOLBOX

You have learned so many new styles that will make your own hand lettering unique! Here is a recap of all that you have mastered in this book:

LESSON 3: THICK AND THIN

THICK + THIN

LESSON 4: CIRCULAR

CIRCULAR

LESSON 5: TALL

TALL

LESSON 6: CHANGING THE CONNECTION

CHANGING THE CONNECTION

LESSON 7: BRUSH PEN

BRUSH PEN

LESSON 8: SLANTED ANGLE

SLANTED ANGLE

LESSON 9: WIDE SPACE

WIDE SPACE

LESSON 18: DOTS INSIDE

DOTS INSIDE

LESSON 11: PAINT PENS

PAINT
PENS

LESSON 18: DOTS OUTSIDE

Dots
Outside

LESSON 12: CURSIVE SCRIPT

Cursive
Script

LESSON 18: HIGHLIGHTER

HIGH
LIGHTER

LESSON 14: FLOURISHES

Flourishes

LESSON 18: BUBBLES

BUBBLES

LESSON 18: LINES INSIDE

LINES INSIDE

LESSON 18: HEARTS

HEARTS

RESOURCES

Hey there! Here is your additional list of tools, supplies, and locations to buy them.

PLACES TO PURCHASE YOUR TOOLS + SUPPLIES:

Blick: www.dickblick.com

JetPens: www.jetpens.com

Michaels: www.michaels.com

Paper and Ink Arts: www.paperinkarts.com

Paper Source: www.papersource.com

Utrechtart: www.utrechtart.com

OTHER LETTERING PENS:

Art Deco Paint Markers

Bistro Chalk Marker

Micron Pens by Sakura of America

Tombow Fudenosuke Hard Tip brush pen

Tombow Fudenosuke Soft Tip brush pen

Tombow TwinTone Markers

Uchida Marvy Fabric Markers

Uni-ball Gel Pen

OTHER ART SUPPLIES:

Artist's Loft Fundamentals Watercolor Pan Set

Molotow Grafx Art Masking Liquid Pump Marker

Princeton Art Brush Co series 4350 round paint brush

Rhodia Writing Pad

Strathmore Bristol Paper

Strathmore Marker Paper 500 Series

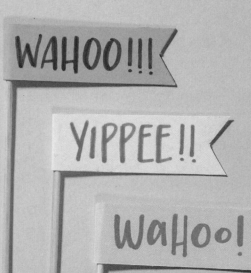

PLACES TO PURCHASE SUPPLIES FOR PROJECTS:

Amazon: www.amazon.com

Etsy: www.etsy.com (stickers, washi tape)

Jam Paper: www.jampaper.com (envelopes, stickers)

Jo-Ann Fabric and Crafts: www.joann.com; and local stores (ribbon, string)

Hobby Lobby: www.hobbylobby.com (wood dowels and other crafts)

Home Depot and Lowe's: www.homedepot.com and www.lowes.com; and local stores (wood, painter's tape, chalk paint, clear mattespray [Minwax Polyurethane Aerosol spray])

Michaels: www.michaels.com (wood, picture frame, ribbon)

Office Max and Staples: www.officedepot.com and www.staples.com (sticky notes, binder, blank tags)

Party City: www.partycity.com; and local stores (balloons)

Save On Crafts: www.save-on-crafts.com (wood)

Totebag Factory: www.totebagfactory.com (tote bags)

USPS: www.usps.com (postage)

Zazzle: www.zazzle.com (postage)

OTHER BOOKS FOR ADDITIONAL LEARNING:

Art Lab for Kids by Susan Schwake

Hand Lettering 101 by Chalkfulloflove

Handwriting Without Tears by Jan Olsen

Happy Mail by Eunice & Sabrina Moyle

How to Draw Modern Florals by Alli Koch

Let's Make Some Great Art by Marion Deuchars

The Art of Cursive Handwriting by Jenny Pearson

THANK YOU!

To the team at Running Press: Julie Matysik, my editor, I am sending the biggest hugs of gratitude. Thank you for wanting me to be here. Susan Van Horn, the book designer, once again, thank you. I'm truly lucky to have gotten to work with you on both of my books and appreciate more than I can express how we are able to work together. Thank you, as well, to those at Hachette Book Group. And, of course, Shannon Connors Fabricant, for finding me and bringing me on board this great team.

To Ikaika, the photographer: over ten years ago we were sitting in a classroom together and now we are here. Enough said. Thank you for allowing me to make sure we got the right shot, keeping me calm, and being a true friend.

To Kaleigh, hand model and cool girl extraordinaire: thank you for being a trouper. You not only are a great model, but, more importantly, you are kind, thoughtful, and a joy to be around. I especially loved when we would start singing songs out loud together!

To Mint Studio: thank you for letting me make your studio my home base for the photoshoot, and for helping me get the younger girls together for the mini-workshop!

To the Winstons: you are my inspirational family. Ever Winston, I want you to know that as a nine-year-old girl you helped give me the confidence to write this book. I will continue to support you in anything you set your creative heart on; dream big, sister.

And to my family and friends: thank you for loving me through this whole process. You were there when I needed it most, and I appreciate all the support. I am who I am because of the people in my life.

xo, Nicole

INDEX

ABOUT NICOLE

NICOLE MIYUKI SANTO is a freelance artist, graphic designer, and teacher. Since 2015, she has taught in-person hand-lettering workshops to students of all ages. She is a kind spirit and truly believes that everyone, kids and adults included, can enjoy using their own two hands to create. Her work has been featured in numerous publications, including *Martha Stewart Magazine*, and she is the author of *By Hand: The Art of Modern Lettering*. Nicole lives in Los Angeles, California. Visit her online at nicolemiyuki.com or on Instagram @nicolemiyuki.